The Freshmen
Unzipped

To Jamie Dean and Harvey Cole
And Sinead McMenamin and Sorca Gill

The Freshmen Unzipped

Derek Dean

MERLIN
PUBLISHING

First published in 2007 by
Merlin Publishing
Newmarket Hall, St Luke's Avenue,
Cork Street, Dublin 8, Ireland
Tel: +353 1 4535866
Fax: +353 1 4535930
publishing@merlin.ie
www.merlinwolfhound.com
Contact Derek Dean at www.derekdean.com

Text © 2007 Derek Dean
Editing, Design and Layout © 2007 Merlin Publishing
except
photographs courtesy of the individuals noted in the picture sections

ISBN 978-1-903582-77-0

A CIP catalogue record for this book is available from the
British Library.

10 9 8 7 6 5 4 3 2 1

Typeset by Gough Typesetting Services
Cover Design by Graham Thew Design
Printed and bound by Creative Print and Design Ltd, UK

Contents

Foreword

In a windblown corner of the north-west of Northern Ireland lie the city of Derry and the town of Strabane. Fourteen miles apart and cut off from their natural Donegal hinterland, these two communities are often considered notoriously cantankerous and psychologically stateless. The people are edgy. Stressed at being left out of things and economically frustrated by the impossibility of their geographical situation, many residents of Strabane and Derry have often found themselves having to make the best of a raw deal.

During the late fifties and early sixties, despite hugging the Donegal border, neither community felt much sense of identification with the Republic of Ireland, lumbered as the 'Free State' was by its own considerable economic problems. The South was not seen then as the prosperous land it is today. Not even so much as a squeak from any tiger.

Nor did the people of Derry or Strabane seem inclined to identify with the state of Northern Ireland. It is sad but true to say that the Unionist government in Stormont took little interest in what was happening in this part of its bailiwick and even seemed to take a certain amount of pleasure in acting accordingly.

Consequently, many of the people in Strabane and Derry felt neither British or Irish. They were on their own, independent – like living in a Monaco without the money.

Having the worst male unemployment rate in Western Europe didn't help much. People had to fall back on their natural talents. Boxing, football and the playing of music were often the only means of providing a young man with a step up the ladder. It is therefore no coincidence that the showband was born here.

Despite fierce speculation and heated opinion it is generally acknowledged that the first showband in Ireland was the Clipper Carlton from Strabane. Other heated claims come from Derry, maybe because the city embraced the showband culture so completely and readily. It was said that a man could not throw a stone in Strabane or Derry without hitting someone who was either a member of a showband or desperately trying to join one.

There were sound reasons why either Derry or Strabane invented the showband.

For generations young girls from Donegal had migrated to Derry and Strabane destined for the sweatshops of the shirt factories. They brought with them a fondness for music that filtered down through the generations. (My own mother was hired in the 'Rabble' in Derry in 1919. As the old folks say, a tune was seldom off her lips.)

The American base in Derry was hugely influential. Affluent Americans strolling confidently through grey, grimy streets became our heroes and role models, backed up by the movies we saw in the local fleapits. We saw our Americans for real, and they passed the test. That also meant rock 'n' roll. The Yanks could buy the latest American hits in their PX (a military store on the base where American goods were on restricted sale) months before they became available in Britain.

Again, these records filtered down to us. This fuelled the psyche of successful, Americanised showbands such as the Johnny Quigley Showband, and, indeed, the Clipper Carlton before them, the eyes and ears of Strabane being equally alert.

There was also a long-standing tradition of young men joining brass bands, in much the same way as miners joined colliery bands in the North of England, except that we had no coal – just Dole.

So, the combination of young men with nothing else to do and nothing to lose, the ready availability of the latest American rock 'n' roll sounds, a native love of music coupled with a tradition of brass players – all contributed to the birth of the 'showband'.

In the midst of all this, the young Derek McMenamin was maturing and soaking up what we used to call the 'vibes'.

Born in Strabane, he spread his wings, morphed into Derek Dean and, with Billy Brown, formed a vital part of the Freshmen from Ballymena, unanimously acknowledged as the most talented showband of them all.

The Freshmen were head and shoulders above the rest. People admired the slickness of Dickie Rock's Miami, the energy and enthusiasm of Brendan Bowyer's Royal Showband, the 'blokeishness' of the Capitol Showband, the military precision of Eileen Reid and the Cadets, the looniness of the Dixielanders, the vocal gymnastics of Joe Dolan, the sentimentality of Big Tom and the bullfrog croak of Larry Cunningham, but it was given that the Freshmen were special.

The band was particularly expert at reproducing the masterworks of the Beach Boys. I was living in Dublin as a member of a band called the Chessmen when the Beach Boys released the classic 'Good Vibrations'. The initial reaction of my fellow showband musicians was not to praise the record, but rather to wonder if even the Freshmen would be capable of reproducing this complicated opus live, without benefit of a safety net or artificial aids, in front of two thousand sweaty punters.

We knew that the test would come when the Freshmen played the prestigious Monday night dance in the Television Club in Dublin, a gig notorious in that all the 'heads' were there, Monday being the night most showband musicians were off duty.

Everybody gathered to see if the Freshmen could pull it off.

The band did not keep us waiting. Nor did they disappoint.

'Good Vibrations' was perfectly reproduced. It took our breath away. As if someone had put the record on backstage and pushed it through the speakers.

But we didn't really appreciate how good the Freshmen were until the Beach Boys themselves eventually made it to Dublin and made extremely heavy weather of their back catalogue, 'Good Vibrations' being the song they had most trouble with.

But the Freshmen were more than just a copy

band. They were capable of moving on.

Musical ambition was generally fatal in the showband business of the sixties and seventies and so it was that the Freshmen eventually crashed and burned.

More of this anon, and also about the late Billy Brown, surely one of the most original talents on these islands. Although I saw Derek Dean often, I never shared a stage with him. However, I did play in a band with Billy. When he left the Freshmen he formed a number of outfits. One of them was called Brown and O'Brien, a collaboration with ex-Real McCoy singer Mike O'Brien. I was the bass guitarist. It was time well spent.

I benefited from and marvelled at Billy Brown's unique musical gift. He also told me much about Derek and the crazy, glory days, his stammer worsening as his enthusiasm heightened.

But why should I tell you about the Freshmen?

Let Derek Dean do the unzipping...

Gerry Anderson
2007

Introduction

At the last count, 47 musicians had played in the band called the Freshmen. I met them all except one and probably remember about half of them. Some stand out and will be remembered, to a greater or lesser degree, by those who danced and partied in the Ireland of the 1960s and early 1970s.

It was a long time ago now, but there was one Freshman who was to make a mark, not only on my musical awareness but on my whole sense of being, of living, of values, of sinning and of celebrating life itself. His name was Billy Brown.

As Bill was a captivating presence, there were others who passed and were hardly noticed. One such, in particular, deserves mention and the tale in the telling might give you a flavour of what lies ahead.

I met this particular individual walking down Grafton Street in Dublin on a Monday afternoon in the mid-seventies. He introduced himself with the "Jaysus Bigman, good to see you are you goin' for a pint?" routine. I nodded in reply, not too bothered about never having seen this fellow drinker before. Safely seated in a corner of Davy Byrne's pub, he followed me round and all the while kept up a litany of amazing facts about the Freshmen.

My paranoia was growing as he rambled on about how good the band was playing at the time, the programme of songs we were doing, how well Bill was playing and so on. This was no ordinary fan. Not only did he know the venues we were doing, but he was also clued in about the crowds we were getting at the gigs.

It's the taxman, my fevered mind was telling me. This bastard is about to land me with a gigantic bill for the whole band and all this shite talk is the preamble to the final denouement, the dirty wanker.

At the time, the word in the business was that this scourge of all working men was calling upon the bands, one by one, and taking their vans, suits, instruments – everything he could lay his hands on – in lieu of money if your affairs weren't in order. Ours, certainly, were in a state of chaos.

More gargle, and by now I was onto the double vods with no chaser and the sweat was coming out from under the collar. The paranoia was getting worse and it was taking a mighty effort to stop crying. I had, somehow, been set up. I was going to take the fall for the whole band; they all lived in the North and they wouldn't even come to visit me in jail. We probably owed millions.

Your man was at the bar getting in another round, and when he arrived back at the table I just couldn't take anymore. As he left the two drinks down on the table and settled down to drink his, I lurched forward and grabbed him by the throat. Squeezing him by his Adam's apple, I shouted into his terrified face: "OK prick head, who the fuck are you? Where are you from and what do you want off me?"

"Gurgle gurgle, aaargh," was all the poor man

could get out.

By now the other drinkers were standing well back, as a bar-room brawl seemed about to erupt.

"Speak up, you bastard son of Satan, whore's melt of a sheep-shaggin' father. Who sent you?"

I had to let go of his throat, as the word coming through to my demented head was that a tax bill was one thing, but murder in Davy's was surely another.

He sat back down on his chair and looked at me fearfully, while massaging his neck with his hand.

"Holy Jaysus Bigman, are you serious, do you not know who I am?" he croaked.

"Speak up or I swear I'll do serious damage," the paranoia now in full flow. There was a drop of drink left in my glass and I milled it.

Still holding and rubbing his throat, the impostor uttered: "I've been drumming with the band for the past three weeks. I was speaking to you only last night in Cavan and said I would meet you today for a drink."

What could I do or say?

I was beat. The blackout blues had won again. Here was a man I had sung in front of for weeks and, at that very moment in time, I had never seen him before. No wonder he knew the venues, the crowds and the general tales of life on the road that all travelling bands encounter. He was the fuckin' drummer. How stupid was I?

In a frantic attempt to regain some credibility I roared: "Ah bejaysus man, I had you there, didn't I?"

But by now the wounded minstrel was backing away. There was a look of serious distrust in his eyes and, to win him back, I started to pretend it had all been a big joke. I didn't want the rest of the boys to hear this, as my stock at the time was running fairly low.

"And a great drummer you are too!" I shouted, or something equally pathetic, as he headed for the door.

But he was gone, the bar had fallen quiet again and I was left with nothing else to do than finish the business I had come into the bloody place to achieve in the first place ... get blotto.

I don't think the poor man ever played with the band again.

So you see what I mean when I say that there are some members of the band that I don't remember. I obviously didn't remember them at the time.

As with musicians, so with roadies. Or road managers, as they preferred to be called. We had all sorts of individuals behind the wheel, humping gear, getting drink, getting drunk, lining up one-night escorts and various other bits and pieces, like selling records or dumping them. This latter practice involved getting shot of merchandise that had been bought on behalf of the band to manipulate the chart standings of the day. Everyone was at it and it's still done to this day, but in a much more sophisticated manner. The roadies were a hardy lot. One of them was profoundly deaf and another had a wife he called 'Jaws'.

I think they had their own union and would always be guaranteed to tell you anything but the truth. I remember one time in an overnight hotel a roadie started a hullabaloo with myself and a few others. He broke all the main windows in the residents' lounge, as he threw full bottles of beer at my head. He then started on the furniture. There was no consoling the man. He seemed to believe that his girlfriend had been accompanied to the ladies' toilet by a member of the band. What he imagined he witnessed there never came out, but you can imagine the sort of thing that might have upset him.

At checkout time the following morning we had to pay the previous night's fee, plus a bit more, before we could leave. In those days it was meant to be the band that wrecked hotels, not the roadies. The Freshmen were nothing if not original.

So let me begin by naming the men that most people who knew the Freshmen will remember. Billy, of course, but then there was Sean Mahon, Maurice Henry, Davy McKnight, Torry Megahy and Damien McIlroy. That was the line-up of the band that would go on to make the big time in Ireland and the littler time in the UK and further abroad.

The Freshmen was a recording band whose songs still sound alive in 2007 and whose reputation survived fairly intact in the years since it last performed in anger towards the end of 1981. The band played for presidents and prime ministers and had the great distinction of performing the 'Concert for Peace' at the RDS in the early 1970s. Mícheál Mac Liammóir and Hilton Edwards, the two lover-boy stalwarts of Irish theatre, were involved in that project and it has a story all of its own, which I'll tell you later.

The drug of choice at the time in Ireland was alcohol and the Freshmen had its addicts, like most of the other outfits we met on the road.

The story you are about to read will hopefully

give you an insight into what it was like in a touring band in the Ireland of the 1960s and early 1970s. It will bring you an insider's view of the endless one-night stands – both women and venues – and the many priest-like characters of the day who would rob you blind in the name of the Church renovation fund or the airport for 'somewhere or other' holy fund.

The Freshmen was a mould-breaking harmonic union of well-matched voices and instruments, which came together at the right time and made a small contribution to the development of the pop industry in Ireland.

Having mentioned musicians and roadies, the next category, of which we had more than a few, would be … managers.

Here we had the very cream of Irish managerial talent. The late Peter Dempsey, or the Demp, was the first man to take the reins. He was succeeded by one of the most visionary of Irish promoters, Oliver Barry, a Corkman, who brought out the *craic* in the band and who took us to the top of the tree, where many another would have floundered in a sea of alcohol.

Louis Walsh went on to become a household name himself, in this day and age of celebrity adoration, and his many successes were not an overnight thing.

After Louis, the band was managed by Paul Claffey, another who became a household name, especially in Western households.

And then of course, there were the promoters – mostly men, and some women – who made the whole thing possible by throwing up great monuments to the inventor of cement blocks in every parish in Ireland. Some of these venues were more sophisticated than others. Some were to become legends. Satan himself is reputed to have appeared at a few of them and I saw him quite often myself as I said goodbye to another bottle of something or other after a gig.

It was the time of the pill. The Great Liberation of Irish Womanhood. The old PP could no longer shout about the evils of fornication. Sure this was the time when the casual encounter behind the van or in the back seat of the car was given the OK by the little tablet that blocked conception. Come on girls, get the knickers off, there's dancin' to be done. Seven nights a week and every night like Christmas Eve. Well that's what it seemed like at the time.

And then, there was the music. What a drug. It was as if the whole island had turned on at exactly the same time. All tastes were catered to and fashion followed the notes. Hemlines got shorter, magazines sprang from nowhere and all sorts of new careers were launched. Recording studios appeared overnight and men called engineers came to work in them. Entrepreneurs started record labels and soon there were chart shows on the radio and guys called deejays. Everything American and we loved it.

But back to the Freshmen. If you heard them on a good night, when at least half of them were sober, you would never forget it. Is this not a bit boastful coming from an ever-present member? Not at all. I was their biggest fan. In the early days, before king alcohol took a grip, I would regularly leave the stage to stand down in the crowd and listen to the sound coming from the merry men. It really turned me on and I felt very privileged to be able to go back onstage and sing it out in front of them. And that, dear reader, is the truth of the matter.

It was a young man's dream that somehow got out of hand and turned into every man's nightmare. It is a hilarious story and a sad one too. It brought me to places and occasions I could only ever have dreamed of as a young man in Strabane and put me in touch with some unforgettable people. The Freshmen was a great band to me and, in this telling of its story, I will try and give you a flavour of that greatness. Please read on.

Derek Dean,
October 2007

ONE

The Brethren

The public telephone handset was resting on top of the black money box.

"Is tha yir maun way the baun frae the college there?" it sounded like. I thought it must be a call from Glasgow, or somewhere else in Scotland.

"Whaaaa?"

I was standing in the hallway outside the resident's lounge of St Joseph's Teacher Training College in Belfast and I hadn't been expecting any calls, never mind one from the highest highlands, as this speaker seemed to be calling from.

"It's a baun called Freshmen and they wanney heer yi."

That's funny, I thought, just the day before there was an argument in a poker school about different bands and what distinguished them from each other and the lad from Ballymena had been raving about the Freshmen. I'd never heard of them and, coming from Strabane, I had shouted loud in praise of the original and, in my eyes, unmatched showband Clipper Carlton, or the Clippers as they were known. A few of the lads from Derry were staking claims for The Johnny Quigley Orchestra and it was hard to argue with them, as I had recently heard them in the Pallidrome in Strabane and they were a knock-out. A different style of band to the Clippers, but still very impressive.

It was 1961 and the idea of someone calling me from Scotland was a fairly big deal. I was a bit confused.

"Can you slow down a bit please and say it again?"

"Aye, weer Freshmen and we wanney hear ye and see ye singing."

It was my first introduction to the Ballymena or rather north Antrim accent and it transpired that this man was in the Freshmen, had heard about my college four-piece band and received favourable reports about the singer and wanted to come and hear him sing.

"Fair enough, but we don't have another gig until the end of term and that's about a month away."

The stranger's voice lilted back that this would be no problem, as they would come to the college next day and all I had to do was organise one of the music rooms with a piano and the job would be oxo, or words to that effect. I understood that a few of the Freshmen would be calling the next afternoon after lectures and one of them would play the piano.

But Jaysus, I had never heard an accent like that before. It sounded real corny and country hickish.

Not the kind of vibe you would expect from a laid-back muso who could drive your head slightly off centre. This was the buzz I had to have in those days. I had been singing semi-professionally with bands out of Strabane since my first paying gig in Donegal town at the age of eleven. I recall getting 50 shillings (or 50 bob as it was known), and in 1954 that was a lot of readies for a lad just out of short trousers.

In the early days I just accepted that you stood in front of whoever happened to be behind you, opened your mouth and sang. It was fairly basic stuff. I mean, if you were in the front, they had to be in the back. Keep it simple, eh?

It didn't matter what the instrumentation was in the backline, or what noise or racket they were making, you just sang out really loud and hoped you were getting heard over the trombone, trumpet, piano, saxophone, drums, bass, accordion, banjo, lute, flute, mouth organ or harp. Now, no one outfit would have all of the above in the line-up but you were sure to meet them all if you were singing with different bands each weekend.

There was a recruiting ritual every Sunday morning outside Strabane church after 11 o'clock Mass. The band leaders, serious men who had served their time in the trade, would stand outside the church gates and keep their eye out for whoever they needed for the coming week's work. I say a week, but there were rarely more than two gigs a week: Friday and Sunday nights.

The trick was to walk slowly past the man you had been working for the previous week. Strabane was full of musicians and great singers, so there was no guarantee you would get the nod. But if you did your job, kept your mouth shut after the dance, carried all the gear out to the wagon, sometimes hearse or ice-cream van, and didn't get smart if they got a bit sozzled, then you were on a fairly safe wicket. It was, literally, learning the trade.

Mostly these bands were settled, but if a Cuban bongo player had sailed into Derry docks on one of the Yankee submarines it would be a shame not to give him a chance to display his talents to the masses in the northwest. And the Derry bands, always brilliant, seemed to fare better than the Strabane men when it came to availing of the new influences, both in music and personnel.

It's a widely held belief that the reason Derry has produced so many brilliant musicians is because of the American impact of the submarine sailors, with their early jazz and pop records. They introduced the northwest of Ireland to these disciplines and the Derry men, being no mugs, didn't look a gift horse in the mouth.

Derry laid claim to some of the brightest talents of the day. The McIntyre family, Gary and Joe, were at the forefront of a musical explosion out of the maiden city. The Anderson Brothers weren't far behind and the McCaffreys knew all about makin' head-turning sounds.

In those days the transatlantic eiderdown spread to my hometown and on into Omagh where bands such as the Plattermen were starting up. No country bands, but a vein of hard-core rock 'n' roll, which became the trademark of so many Northern musicians.

One night I got a call to gig with one of the more established outfits in the town. The dance was somewhere in County Down and it involved a fair bit of travel. I just loved getting into the bus of The Jimmy Sturrock Orchestra and Ensemble. I felt like a made man. I was too intimidated to speak on the way to the gig and really there wasn't much talk in the van that night. Nobody in the band seemed aware of how excited I was.

The gear was set up onstage and before the show the trombone player, who was now aware of my excited state mentioned: "Young fella, when you sing these Elvis songs, make sure you stay in the same key for each of them, OK son?"

"Oh sure, sure," I nodded, not really understanding what he was on about, but really looking forward to getting wrapped around a whole bunch of Presley hits. I knew about six of them and it was agreed we would do a medley. The usual stuff, "Hound Dog", "Heartbreak Hotel", "Don't Be Cruel" and some more. All I understood was that I would get the chance to sing every Elvis song I'd ever heard and sing them all at once. Heaven.

I'd never been asked to render Elvis songs before and this was a real treat for a young fella. I sang them all day in St Columb's College at school and to do it now in front of a real band was a moment sublime.

"Don't change the tempo or key, son," whispered Jimmy, the man himself, as I was introduced to the well-filled hall as the special treat for the night.

Gimme that fuckin' mike, I thought, walking to the front of the band. Someone played a chord and off I went.

"Oh baby let me be..."

Followed by total disarray. Not only did I sing every song in the original key and kept jumping scales, but the tempo was as the King had recorded. The advice of not changing key was lost on a lad in frenzy and the hips and legs swayed to tempos that the Sturrock drummer had no chance of staying with. I was in dreamland.

But fair play to Jimmy. I was paid a man's wages as I got out of the van in the wee small hours. The thought of making in a night what most working men made in a week didn't bother me at that particular time. I suppose the morality was washed away with the excitement of it all. It was a question, nonetheless, that I would come back to in the future.

That was the only gig I had with them, all the same. The Orchestra and Ensemble had obviously decided that the young McMenamin lad would learn the biz at someone else's expense. Enough was enough.

In today's lingo it would be called part of the learning curve. To me it was magic *craic*.

And so it continued. In St Columb's College in Derry I formed a little three-piece for a special concert to celebrate something or other and we put a fair effort into presenting a few tunes. There was nothing exceptional about the performance. There was no protest, no campus angst, which was beginning to be exhibited at various educational venues in the rest of Europe and America. The student body seemed to enjoy the show and the only dissenting voice came from the college president, a humpy oul fella who was the bishop's uncle or something (word had it that was why he had the job in the first place). Anyway, his head was stuck firmly up his arse as he mounted the stage and condemned 'Le Jazz Americain'. It was funny really. All the starved boarders had to nod like Homer, in agreement with the boss, or they risked not being fed that night. Also the show had absolutely nothing that could be remotely termed 'jazz'. It wasn't hard to insult young lads who believed they were the bee's knees and we had no reason to believe otherwise.

From St Columb's it was on to St Joseph's Teacher Training College (Trench House, or the Ranch as it was known), to be moulded into young Catholic teachers at the State's expense. Off to Belfast to mix with all the other, mainly disinterested, scholars who had chosen the teaching gig as a means of making the honest dollar.

It was like a five-star hotel to a young lad from Strabane. We freshmen each had our own room and it was lockable. That was the most exciting thing about it. Once inside with the key in your hand, you could keep the hordes outside forever. You could snare a lady, have a band practice, set up a decent poker school or get up to any devilment imaginable.

In the first week I went about organising a band and it wasn't long until we had a fairly passable outfit. The influence was all pop songs, with a leaning to rhythm and blues. Chuck Berry was beginning to take off in the States and we were lucky enough to have obtained a copy of some of his early output. Ray Charles was also on the list, as was Bob Dylan and Don 'Sea of Heartbreak' Gibson. As often as possible, we practised in one of the music rooms until they were locked up at night. We would always be in there batterin' away and there wasn't a night but we would have a crowd of the brethren outside listening and singing along.

The guitar man in the band was from the Antrim

village of Randalstown and it was his brother Damien who had made the call to me arranging an audition for the Freshmen. He had never mentioned his brother or the band and, to tell the truth, I wasn't too pushed either way. We had our own little group and were enjoying the hours spent just doing it. So as I put the head down that night in my room, there was no nervousness or excitement about the morrow's encounter. I slept well.

Three men appeared at the main music room door. Two were fairly ordinary-looking, regular guys but the third was a real mind-blower. It's hard at this remove to describe the impact Billy Brown had on my head when I first saw him swagger towards me with his hand outstretched. I think it was love at first sight. It was definitely amazement and wonder at first sight, as I had never seen such a striking an individual in all my eighteen years on planet earth.

He wore, or rather sported, a very loud black and white check two-piece suit with white shirt and yellow bow tie (the type you tie yourself) and he had the ends of the tie nearly touching in a sort of ultra casual fashion. You could easily identify that this was not of the clip-on variety. His smile was, for want of a better word, beguiling, but there was no deception there. Straight away I could feel the presence of something extra about this man, something special.

His long, wavy-blond hair flicked out easily over the checked jacket and, as he sat down at the piano stool without invitation, my eyes tracked the brown hush puppies as they were planted gently on the pedals of the best piano the Ranch had to offer.

"So there, ah, Derek, what's it to be then?"

By this stage, I hadn't given the other two lads a glance and, when I did, I could see that one of them, David McKnight, the band's drummer, had noticed my fascination with this presence.

Davy was smiling at me as if to say, yeah man, I can see you're gobsmacked and so am I, but you better start singing for him or else we're off.

"What about 'Sweet Little Sixteen'?" I ventured.

The music room, which was intended to hold about six at a push, was by now jam-packed as word spread about the strange man in the suit from this Ballymena band.

"Chuck Berry or Jerry Lee?" He looked up from under his eyelids and the massive head of blondeness.

"No matter, just play it and I'll sing it," was my reply, thinking to myself that this boy really fancies himself; he thinks that whatever way he plays the banana he'll influence my singing. But I liked the nerve.

To the day I die I will never forget what happened next. His hands began to move and the room filled with the most exquisite sound I had ever heard. It was beautiful.

Music jumped from the belly of the piano and you could feel the breeze as it danced past your face and climbed up the walls and walked across the ceiling of the semi-soundproofed room. It settled on the ceiling tiles upside down, before each note jumped back down inside the joanna's heart. And it didn't stop. It continued on and on and I couldn't take my eyes off the flying fingers caressing the keyboard, doing rolls and accentuations and bringing forth a sound that only the pure can attain. It was magic. The primal instinct was to cry. I wanted to laugh and indeed I did, but most of all I hoped that this fantastic moment would never end.

Outside the tabernacle, for that is what it had become, the student body had congregated. If the Pied Piper was inside doing things with special chords that were burning into their brains, then their duty was to follow him. Necks and heads craned for a vantage point and someone opened the door to let the healing wave forms circulate around them. I stood transfixed.

Suddenly, it stopped.

"Or maybe you prefer this," blondie smiled, as he started into the Jerry Lee Lewis version of the poor sixteen-year-old's lament.

Again the small space filled with wondrous sound. But this time it was head-wrecking in an entirely different manner. Gone was the staccato, punchy, hard-fingered demanding anxious lover who must get his way. In his place was a gigolo out on his travels. Travelling up and down the ivories, tickling and teasing with licks and runs that could only have been designed in Hell, but which were being played at that moment by the brightest star the Heavens ever sent to earth. This was the Maestro.

I was dying to sing, but when I closed my mouth to swallow the awe it wouldn't open again to let out the notes. It seemed as if my jaw was locked. But this was merely personal embarrassment. Singing wasn't important with this celebration. More, more, more. Jaysus, this was the first time I'd tasted freedom. And the check suit and blond head just kept playing away and, at the other end of this wonderful scene, Davy

McKnight was still smiling at me.

You see, he had gone through exactly the same experience. It's like standing waiting for a bus in the rain, totally soaked and pissed off, when all of a sudden a UFO lands in front of you and out comes Miss Mars to give you a blowjob. It's kind of like, you weren't expecting this. But now that it's happening, you'll believe in anything.

"So maybe you fancy singin' something else, what?" came the stammering voice as the music came to a halt again.

And with a huge effort, as a Strabane man not wanting to let the town down in front of this amazing talent, I said: "No, I prefer the first arrangement."

"All right so, you lead," says he.

"No, you go, the key is fine, you go again," and with that little bit of banter, I sang my first song accompanied by the late, great Billy Brown. For the first time in my life, I understood what was meant by a driving force.

I really do believe that it was that day I first started to sing. Everything else had been a preparation for this moment. I had spent seven years learning my trade in public and I felt if I never sang in public again, then I could say I had done it with the very best.

By now the Dean of the College had entered the room and, like everyone else, was silent and overawed. We sang for another twenty minutes and time disappeared.

Turning down the lid of the piano with great care, he uttered: "Aye, that'll do so."

I had only ever asked one man, Nat Lofthouse, the Bolton Wanderers and England centre-forward, for an autograph, but as I was about to ask this wonder to sign something or other for me, he ventured the comment: "Aye, you know how to do it OK."

Before anyone could make any requests of this amazing man, Damien McIlroy, who had been absolutely silent during the whole proceedings, came over and asked: "Can you get to Ballymena tomorrow night, the Flamingo Ballroom, for eight o'clock?"

And they were gone. And so was I and the other brethren. Gone in the head. We had witnessed something special and we all knew it.

Two

The Swinging Bird

It belted rain that night in 1963 on the thirty miles to Ballymena from Belfast and, sitting on the back seat of a wonky motorbike getting drenched, as my buddy Christy and I took a shortcut over the Black Mountain, was a mighty night's *craic* indeed.

I remember laughing and promising Christy a big fry when we got there and he giggling too, because we knew we were both flat broke, a normal state for students in any age.

"Screw the fry, I'd settle for dry," he roared from the front of the old Norton.

We rattled the big wooden door of the Flamingo Ballroom at near enough eight o'clock, shivering with the cold and just about able to utter a few words of encouragement to each other.

"Jaysus Christy, yer a real mate, doin' this for me, I definitely owe you big time."

The door opened and we were greeted with a blast of the accent that I had first heard on the phone a couple of days earlier. It was the proprietor of the Flamingo, a friend to every musician who ever played there, Sammy Barr. Sammy owned a real Ulster Scottish, high fallutin', frantic-pitched, unintelligible-to-the-untrained-ear accent, which was lost on the pair of us.

It was dark inside at ground level, bleak and very cold. As he ushered us up the stairs and into the dance floor area, I was able to make out, from the non-stop chatter, the word "towel".

"Good man, that's a great idea, and Christy there wants a fry." I thought to myself that there must be grub somewhere about.

Hearty laughter greeted that notion and as we walked up the ballroom floor in the near darkness, I was able to make out several guys holding instruments. They were all wearing overcoats and the guitar players had their hands in their pockets.

I recognised Davy McKnight behind the drums and Damien on the guitar and, standing in the middle of three brass men, there was Billy. There was a big grand piano onstage, but there was a canvas cover over it. The sheepskin-coated Brown had a sling around his neck, and on the end of the sling was a tenor saxophone.

"I'm Maurice Henry, band leader, thanks for coming down Derek," said the gently spoken second saxophonist.

"And I'm Sean Mahon," shouted the trombone-player, "and that's Torry Megahy on the bass."

The towels duly arrived and I gathered a couple of facts from Maurice as we dried off.

The band was semi-professional and worked about three nights a week. They planned to go professional as soon as possible and Maurice was responsible for getting in the work. Thanking me again for coming down, he asked me to come up onstage to sing a few songs, accompanied by the rhythm section.

Up I went and the three brass men stood in the middle of the floor along with Sammy as I belted into "Sweet Little Sixteen", followed by a version of "I Can't Stop Loving You" and a ballad which was a big favourite at the time, "Love thee Dearest".

I sang to the big clock, which dominated the back wall of the hall, and to Christy who was sitting in a semi-coma just underneath it. I was using the skull-head Shure mike, which was the best money could buy at the time. It had a wire-mesh strip around its belly and it was the weapon of choice for travelling bands all over the world.

I wasn't aware of the backing so much and, to be honest, I was thinking more of the marathon run back to the city on the back of the foundering bike.

Much discussion ensued between the lads on the dance floor and there were the usual banal smiles exchanged onstage. Like the smile in the doctor's surgery, very polite but meaningless. You're never sure if the good doc is going to fill your head with joy, or empty your heart of hope.

Maurice approached and nodded me down to the side of the stage to where he stood.

"We split everything equally. We're a co-op. We divvy up after each night. We all get the same. Every man is responsible for his own instrument, but in the singer's case we don't expect him to buy the PA.

We put so much from each gig into a kitty and that's what we use for ads, suits, photos and stuff like that. The job's yours if you want it."

"Thanks very much, that's dead on, when are you playing again?"

"Saturday night in Ballyclare town hall and if you let Davy know whereabouts in Belfast you're living, then he can pick you up and bring you down."

By this stage I was fairly exhausted with the whole process and couldn't have cared one way or another; I was so cold and by now ravenous. Christy and I were about to head back to the front door, having shook hands and farewelled ourselves as politely as we could, when Sean Mahon spoke up.

Sean was a very proud man and his pride and joy, I was to discover very soon, was the band.

"Wouldn't it be fair of us to let Derek hear the band play a few songs before he heads off? Be bad manners not to really."

"And warm us up as well," ventured Brown.

I walked down to where the bould Christy had remained motionless, and sat down beside him, hoping that this wouldn't take too long.

I heard it for the first time.

If the sound coming out of the piano room in the Ranch on the previous day was awesome, then what jumped down from the stage that night in Ballymena was inspired by Gabriel himself. It had all sorts of mesmeric power. It dried my whole body, it made the cold disappear and, miracle of miracles, it fed the hungry beast inside. I looked at my friend and we burst out laughing simultaneously.

Like a magnet, I was drawn back to the centre of the hall. I was looking at two saxophones, a trombone, a guitar, a bass and drums, but I was listening to a smiling angel tell me that henceforth I would get laid on a regular basis, nightly in fact, there would be no pain and suffering in the world, and that I would be a part of the curative process.

Now the blond sax man Brown had stepped up, with the bell of his horn sunk right into the old steel skull. And for the first time, I heard a sax solo from the heart. From the heart of mankind. His neck stood out in a cone-shaped distortion, and I thought it would surely explode the harder he blew. His eyes rolled in his head and by now I was pinching myself, asking if this was the same man who had made the piano talk just the previous day. But Billy Brown wasn't the only one to demand attention. The trombone of Mahon was belting a bass crescendo of wicked notes and his cheeks puffed promise of more and more to come. Drums, guitars and the brass had just blown my cold away somewhere into the stratosphere when, before I could offer a pathetic round of applause, they were off again. This time a tight foot-stomping version of "Memphis Tennessee" with Davy singing on drums. My feet were tapping, knees knocking, and fingers clicking all the way down the line of my soul.

"Jaysus, Christy, these boys have just offered me a job. Holy Jaysus."

This time there was no wait for applause; I just let out a mighty roar, and was laughing with tears in my eyes.

The third wall of sound, an instrumental called "Tequila", ended abruptly as Sammy the Goodheart arrived back upstairs from the kitchen with a massive tray of his famous hot dogs. Now the deal was really done. We all agreed that there were some times ahead and that this band would surely take the world by storm.

"We only have a Morris Commercial at the minute, but we will have our own luxury coach soon," enthused Sean Mahon.

I didn't once think of any money that would be made. All I could think of was standing in front of this magic band and having a go. As I child I'd watched the Clipper Carlton fill up at the petrol station opposite my home on the Bridgend, and ever since then I'd longed to play in a big band. A band that would make you proud, they way I was proud of the Clippers just because they came from Strabane.

I don't quite remember the spin home on the motorbike. It had stopped raining, but either way it didn't matter. Here I was, a horny lad of 19 and I'd just been offered and accepted, a job with the greatest band I had ever heard. I was about to begin the greatest adventure a man can take. Who knew where it would lead?

THREE

The Early Days

The showbands burst onto the scene when there was no scene to burst onto.

There were no record shops, no recording studios, no record labels, no TV programmes, no TV, no dedicated radio programmes, no nightclubs, no music charts, no glossy pop magazines, no publicists, no disc jockeys, no promoters, no electric guitars, no electric keyboards, no teenagers and not much fun.

But it was all coming.

This infrastructure was non-existent in 1960, except for a few isolated ballrooms around the country, but it began to emerge slowly. There was a dancehall building boom throughout the early 1960s and their number actually quadrupled in five years. The big city venues in Belfast, Dublin, Cork, Derry and Limerick also saw a major increase in the growth and development of their nightlife-nookie parlours and devil's pit attraction holes.

The Clippers didn't have an electric bass guitar. Part of their act involved Art O'Hagan and his brother Fergie, he of the golden bass voice, playing the upright double bass and swinging it around in circles, riding it, rocking it, sitting on it and, the odd time, being supported by it when the band was really cooking. It was wonderful to behold and the sight thrilled dancers up and down the land. What you don't know about you don't miss, and no one in Irish music had even heard the name Fender, never mind owning the instrument, which, more than any other, would become synonymous with pop music around the world.

The same principle held true for the Johnny Quigley All-Stars. From Derry, these men were rock 'n' roll incarnate. There must have been about ten of them in the band and anytime I ever saw them, my jaw dropped.

They were most accomplished rockers and carried a brass section that would have been at home in a big band. They had a couple of saxes, a tenor, a baritone, an alto, a trumpet and a trombone. Whenever they wanted to really liven up a hall, they would use two trumpets and this they just accepted as run of the mill. Mighty men indeed. Whereas the Clippers were a real showband with the emphasis on the 'show', the Quigley band was more into a cross of Derry rock and American roll. They used to open up their act with a song by the Coasters: "Baby That is Rock and Roll". The singer's basso profundo voice would drawl in a Birmingham Alabama accent, the evangelical opening lines of the Leiber and Stoller classic ditty:

> In the beginning there was nothing but rock,
> but then somebody invented the wheel,
> and so we all began to roll.

There followed a mind-blowing live version of pure ecstasy. And the night would be full of pure, pulsating, head-wrecking, rhythmic disturbance. By this I mean the music got in the way of the Serpentine Imperative, that of attending to the hungry demands of the throbbing monster somewhere down the leg of your trousers. There was a constant battle between the musical aesthetic and the sexual athletic. It was a case of not being able to take your attention off the stage and not wanting to miss out on the bounty gracing the dance floor. On a blissful night both appetites were sated, but a hard rockin' band was a major consolation, on many's a night, for a soft cockin' man.

For anyone not around at the time, the accepted etiquette in halls was a fairly hilarious and nationally accepted ritual. The women lined up on one side of the battlefield and the lads on the other. As soon as the drummer counted in the band and the song began, this line of horns would stroll, expectantly, across the neutral territory between the two lines and ask the target to dance. Sometimes the stroll would resemble a stagger and the lady being invited to foxtrot, waltz, smooch and jive would muster up the courage to refuse. But this was the exception. A man would have needed to be in desperate shape to be turned down.

The real business of scoring a goal, of course, was in the hands of the women. The "Ladies' Choice" tactic was a strategy that they used to signify their true intentions to would-be suitors. It wasn't unusual for a man to ask an intended out to dance for a couple of sets and still not work up the courage to invite her up for a mineral or down for a bit of the other, depending on the make and shape of the individuals concerned. But all serious intent was disclosed if she were to approach and extend the invitation to stroll the boards.

This was the confirmation. If you didn't proposition her one way or another during this declaration of stated interest, then either you weren't bothered, or else you didn't have the price of the mineral. But in most cases the job was oxo and a good night and, in some cases, it has to be said, a good future, lay ahead. Maybe the odd woman would have made the first verbal move herself, but that would have been extremely rare. I'm not going to bore you with a lot of dilly talk about the number of happy marriages that came about as a result of loving encounters at dances in the 1960s. Where else could they have happened?

All this took place on the cusp of the advent of the contraceptive pill. This event did more to swell the ranks of dancers and party animals than all the records ever recorded. Once the problem of actually getting hold of it was sorted by a converted sisterhood, then the next big problem was what to do with it and where could it be done. And what better place, seeing as they weren't welcome in the pubs, than the dance halls of Ireland.

Women of all ages suddenly discovered that not only could they now trip the light fantastic, they could lie down in it, get laid in it, scream their heads off in it or be disappointed by it, which was more likely, and not end up pregnant. Liberation was on the way. Never before in the history of "he-in' and she-in'" (Ulster dialect) had such opportunity for love presented itself.

This was light years away from the slavery and enslavement that has been condoned and approved of by the men in collars and dresses for generations. As one, the womenfolk of Ireland rose up and rode into a new sunset of sexual liberation. They just rode away.

There seems to be a misconception about the origins of the massive crowds of people who danced the night away to the sounds of the fabulous showbands in the 1960s and early 1970s. The misunderstanding is based on the false assumption that hordes of Irish people somehow got a dance bug, all at the same time, and travelled the length and breadth of the nation to exorcise its unyielding demands. It has been mooted that band after band magically appeared in a haze of creative enlightenment and that the denizens of this wonderful realm traversed the land in expensive forays to hear them play their mesmerising music.

These incredible outfits were springing up in every town, village, hamlet and crossroads all over the country. They just kept coming and the people, bedazzled by this entire symphony, just kept following in a Pied-Piperesque, manic spell.

The reality is that exactly the opposite was the case.

Women, equipped with their little secret silent partner-in-joy, decided that it was time to let rip. They headed out in their thousands and where they went the men followed. Every night of the week,

North and South, the pattern was repeated. With the exception of Saturday night in the Republic. This was a blank date in the showband calendar because of Mass on a Sunday morning. That would change in time, as this was only the start of an unstoppable social revolution. It was the beginning of the end for the religious rearguard, which had for so long hammered home their obsessive sermon, that morality was, largely based on something between your legs.

The lads and lassies, in hired buses and cars, loved every minute of it. Get locked, get laid and maybe the chance of a bit of decent music at the same time. This was the end of the *ceilí* in the kitchen and the time was coming fast when men's splendid isolation in the pubs would be a thing of the past.

There's a song "Can't Stop Blues", and it opens with the couplet:

> It's hard to stop at ground level
> When you're shooting out of hell

This summed up what was going on with the emerging force of Irish womanhood.

The jury, however, is out on the question of the pill, in relation to did it or did it not bring wagonloads of easy sex to the bands of musicians, travelling up and down the land.

Since a lad of fourteen, I had experienced the differing effect of being up there, singing in the spotlight, and being down there, dancing in the crowd.

It was at a dance in Killybegs, a major fishing port in Donegal, that I first tasted the bliss.

> I'll never forget the first time,
> She was twenty-three, I was five past nine

are the opening lines of a ditty called "Juicy Lucy". That wasn't her name, but she was a fisherman's wife or girlfriend and I had been belting it out at the local dance with a gather-up from Strabane. That is, if you can belt it out with an accordion, a fiddle, a drum kit that consisted of a snare with just one cymbal, and an unamplified, damaged keyed piano.

I was a big lad and she sat all night on the stage front and smiled every so often. Like all fourteen year olds, I was fascinated at the thought and totally intimidated at the prospect of 'doing it'. This was real man's stuff and although I was the size of a man, I was really a wean on the inside. I was also carrying certain strange beliefs, which had been inculcated into my eager mind by the lads and lasses in the collars and dresses while still at primary school.

"Every time you masturbate, you kill a child; a baby dies," was the stuff they filled our heads with, about age ten or eleven, the very age the serpent was posing a nightly problem. Jaysus, they rammed this shit down into your brain, until I ended up feeling like a mass murderer who couldn't stop. Looking back, I realise it was an appalling stance for them to adopt, but that was the business they were in. Keep the people down, don't give them free rein to express themselves and, for the love of God, don't allow them to express any bit of self-love that might come in a bit handy when things got a bit low.

It was in the back of my excited head that this lovely lady might be willing to experiment with me, as I sat down beside her for a talk. I think that was as far as I really wanted it to go. I would maybe get close and then she'd baulk and all would be well. But she was having no half measures. She was fairly clear about me accompanying her to the side of the van and we could have a "chat" before her lift back home. Little did she know that we travelled in a hearse, but it wouldn't have mattered, so loud was the horn.

My heart was thumping, my cock was jumping and it walked out the side door in front of me. I remember thinking at the time that it was like the stiff indicator that stuck out of the side of a Morris Minor motor. It was pointing the way and surely, I imagined, was apparent to all and sundry in the ballroom. Not that anyone was paying attention at the side of the van, round the back of the hall.

I fumbled and foostered. She unzipped and lifted. I fumbled some more and the serpent was so stiff I could hardly get it to leave the bastard trousers. She insisted on helping and her touch practically drove the beast wild. Before I knew it, the confounded thing was in the hottest, most heavenly environment it had ever known. Warm, welcoming, wonderful and wicked – and very quick.

No sooner had this mighty fun begun than the hysterical mamba let out his yell of triumph, of manhood, his resounding roar of spine tingling delight. It was a Samson moment. It was a statement of release. My whole body shivered with the electric energy which shot through and up and out of my cock. Joy beyond belief for me. But, I'm sure, wild disappointment in the knickers of the fisherwoman.

But she was a sympathetic woman and didn't show her dissatisfaction. Although I dreamed of her every night and relived the whole adventure over and over again, to the accompaniment of the one-handed polka, I never did meet her again, in the flesh.

FOUR

The First Dip

"And here, ladies and gentlemen, at this part of the show, we'd like you to put your hands together and welcome our new lead singer, Derek McMenamin." He kind of stumbled on the McMenamin bit the way most people did at the time, but who cared about that? We had agreed beforehand that, not having had a proper rehearsal, I should just do a couple of the songs we had busked at the auditions.

Out I ran and grabbed the old steel skull from the mike stand, held it in my right hand and began to rock. I was wearing my only suit; a brown two-piece job, which had been worn so often it had gone shiny at the seat. It fitted in nicely with the brown checks the other lads sported, but none of that was important. It was a night to let the beast out. Out to have a look at what the lads had promised was the best talent in any hall in the North. But I didn't

see any of them. I saw the other guys laughing and
smiling as I jumped around the small stage. If they
didn't know beforehand what they were getting
themselves into when I signed up, well they certainly
knew now. This wasn't a music room or a cold,
empty ballroom in the dark of a winter's night. This
was live action. Take no prisoners. Half measures
avail us nothing, so let's get rockin'. That was my
genuine thank you to the fabulous musicians behind
me. I would give this gig everything I had and start
out the way I meant to continue.

By the third number I threw off the heavy
jacket and now stood singing my head off, wearing
a half-white shirt and a hard-on. No time to feel
embarrassed. It was the heat and the music that were
driving me on. All too soon I was on my last number
for the night and, looking to my right, I caught sight
of the line of three brass men, heads down. They were
blowing up a thunderous riff and moving with its
push and pull, the way an early wave comes into the
strand; it thunders in and then rushes out again and
its sound is different every time. Its notes are lodged
into the seashells and they present themselves for
evermore to those who care to listen. That's what
was happening to my brain. These men were blowing
a pattern, an electrical circuit, into my overheated
head. And it just got louder and louder. They didn't
look towards me. They were letting me get on with
whatever it was I was up to, but they were off about
business of a far more serious nature. The riff had
caught hold. Critical mass had been attained. On
my left the guitars were keeping it hot and simple.
And behind me the steady, pulsating beat; the never-
ending pounding of a pagan rhythm, beating into

my psyche, was relentless.

My heart was pumping and jumping in my chest and the hard-on was jumping and thankfully not pumping in my trousers. I began to jump. Up as high as I could. I thought I might be able to fly. Surely all the power of the music would allow me lift off. I was up there already and I wanted the body to follow, but I didn't quite make it.

Rattle, rattle, schlapp, schlapp on the drums and it ended with a sustained chord from the brass, with Billy playing a counter riff all over and around the two men holding notes. It was over.

The men on horns bowed, looked and pointed to me. I stood frozen to the spot. The audience was clapping and, for the first time, I heard a young voice scream. I was flabbergasted. Of course I wanted to do it all again, but it was over. And the best part was – it was only just beginning.

I knew all about pagan rhythm from an early age in Strabane. As a kid, I would go to the parochial hall in the Bridgend on a Sunday night and be fascinated at the antics of the local priest who diligently patrolled his patch. Couples who danced too close for his comfort were dealt with in a very effective manner. He would walk up behind the man and deliver a mighty slap across the back of his lusty head. It was the Catholic proclamation of purity. "No mickey-dancing in my fuckin' hall", was the message from Father Taliban, "Or I'll beat the shit out of you". The sad thing about it was that he always got away with this selective slapping. He was never stretched out on his arse with a hefty blow from an irate punter, but those were the times that were in it.

If that was the straitjacket of morality that

pertained in Strabane, I imagined that it must have been the same everywhere else. It never occurred to me that it would be any different in other areas of an ultra-conservative wee country. There was a sense that all religions were scared to death by a horny man and they would go to any length to kill off this evil. Sexual freedom seemed like a major threat to the men in skirts and dresses, to the foot soldiers and their bosses who expected young lads to kiss their rings. Just at Confirmation, of course.

And so it was accepted. It was definitely not Christian-like to mickey-dance. It was obviously pagan. And in Ballyclare that night, I was feeling like a big savage chieftain.

"Well done big man," said Maurice as the band came off stage.

"Now get out there and chat to the punters."

And that was that. I felt like all my birthdays had come at once and I was still drinking in the buzz of playing and singing with this heart-stopping band, but the leader was only interested in the PR. I was walking on a cloud of steamy horn and as I went back onto the stage, soaked shirt and all, there was a mini-shuffle of hot female bodies in my direction. King of all Ireland. That's how I felt.

The fact that my face wasn't on the photographs I started handing to the faithful didn't matter.

Included in the photo was the one Freshman I never got to meet. He was the original singer, a lad by the name of Barney who had a falling out with Maurice over something or other and decided to throw his hat at it. I heard he was a singer of note and of great notes, but I could only feel gratitude to him for his generous action in having a row with

Maurice. It was fairly harmless apparently, but it was certainly paying big dividends for me.

I made eye contact with each smiling face as I wrote "Derek McMenamin, vocalist" on the back of each card. Promises were exchanged with each set of eyes and the meaning of mine were, "If we can't get it on tonight then there's always the next time." This was every young man's dream. This was every grown man's dream. A host of golden daffodils all seemingly available and all with no strings attached. There was only the prospect of an encounter; no "I love you" rituals, no "we have to meet again" promises, just a manic urge to sate the serpent.

The other lads were engaged in the same holy work, each with his own set of dedicated followers. The last time I'd had a feeling like this was as a lad in Strabane, progging. The word is not in dictionaries, but if you were brought up in the town, when the time was right we all went progging: standing uninvited in an orchard full of beautiful looking apples and pears and just grabbing as many as you could fit in your pockets and in your upturned jumper. Always, of course, on the lookout for the unfortunate owner, who had been done yet again.

But here in Ballyclare, there were no owners in sight. No mammies or daddies, and certainly no chaperones. And the orchard was bulging with ripe fruit.

"Derek, Derek over here," she shouted, and like a flash I was there.

"Sign my arm please, and can you give me a lift home?"

It was the serpent who replied in the affirmative, even though I didn't have a car.

I'd had my fun and now it was his turn. I suppose fair is fair.

FIVE

From Ballyclare to Strabane

Before long I had rehearsed enough songs to ensure that I sang every second one in a four- or five-hour set. Seems a lot nowadays, but that's how long a gig lasted then. It would be from nine in the evening to one o'clock the following morning on a soft night, or it could run from nine to two, which was inevitably more common. No relief bands meant that you had to have a very substantial repertoire, and most nights we would play instrumentals for the first hour or so. Anything to keep a sound going while the punters were preparing for action.

In those days it was unheard of for women to go into bars and it was only the lads who had the pleasure of filling up with liquid courage before the off. There didn't seem to be any great protests about this state of affairs, and the thought of ladies mingling with the warriors in a dirty pub was generally frowned upon. Ireland's virtue would not be sullied by its lady folk supping the devil's brew in public. It was the same North and South, but there was an odd sighting of a loose woman drinking in pubs reported, and noted, in some Northern towns. And the Freshmen were happily breaking new ground all over the wee six.

I say all over the North because, as of yet, the band hadn't made it to a date across the border, but all hands were talking about "breaking the South" soon. We had no manager and Maurice was responsible for bookings.

One time he had an offer of a gig in Kilrea, County Derry from the parish priest, on condition that the band change its name. Freshmen was "inappropriate, with sexual overtones", so he suggested the "Seven Towers Showband". As Ballymena was the town of the seven towers, that would be acceptable to all. What's the old saying about it all being in the mind? Well, we didn't get round to playing Kilrea, but in the next twelve months we visited every town, village and hamlet in the province. There was a circuit of sorts, and each time we played a venue the crowd would be bigger than before and a fellow would be keeping his eye out for new *craic*. Literally.

Life was good and the studying at college didn't suffer too much, as it was a fairly cushy regime. It didn't take much effort to coast through the lectures and, anyway, most of the band work took place at weekends. There was always money for cigarettes and dating. There were no drugs at the time on the music scene, except for a few times when some of the lads who were driving took a few purple hearts, and as I didn't drink there was always a bit of money left over to hand into the house at home. It was always welcome and life at 18 couldn't be better. A car was needed, of course, but that wouldn't take long, surely.

We always travelled to gigs in the van; our old Morris Commercial had a panel installed roughly a third of the way along her length to hold the gear. Between the back double doors and the wooden panel rested speakers, mike-stands, amplifiers, suits and anything else a touring band needed to survive. Between the panel and the driver's seat at the front was an inverted U-shaped bench-seat, which faced the sliding door at the side of the old junker. Five Freshmen sat in this hellhole, with Maurice and Torry, the only insured drivers, up front. You were guaranteed a sore arse when you arrived to play and maybe you might surrender a few bob en route as well, if you weren't too lucky at the poker school. Fairly normal stuff for a travelling band, and most nights the banter was fairly creative going to and even better coming home, as the serpent snuggled back into passive mode after a mini-outing.

Roadies, or gear-humpers, were unheard of at that time. When you got to the gig there was the unavoidable hassle of carrying the stuff into the hall, up onto the stage and setting it up. Then there would be a soundcheck of sorts and if there was something that someone wasn't too sure about, then we would have a quick run over.

The potential for major hassle happened when it came to loading the oul van up again at the end of the gig.

Dismantling and rolling up sticky, wet mike leads, carrying it all out of the hall and putting it to bed, was a most resented task. It wasn't work for an adrenalin-pumping man. Should you be off about your work of trying to persuade a young lady that your mutual needs were Heaven-sent and ordained for fulfilment that very night and have the misfortune to arrive back at the van, having kept it waiting, then woe betide you. A right bollicking would be all yours.

The other lads had to go to work early the next day and they were all the time complaining that they would have to go full-time professional. Maurice was married and he had a couple of kids to support, but married or not it was a hassle. I couldn't imagine what it was like for the boys to get out of the Morris and maybe get a couple of hours' kip before reporting for work in a factory in Larne, which was where Damien and Billy soldiered. Sean had to drive on to Downpatrick and then back to Belfast to sell car parts. So their desire to be part of a full-time professional band was not just a meritorious badge of pride, but also something of a necessity for their sanity. Perhaps had they known about the perils of life on the road, seven nights a week, they might have reconsidered their options, at least from a work point of view, but just then the day job wasn't a runner. Particularly hard on working men was the dreaded nine to two in the morning, marathon gig. Five hours to be filled before unhooking the gear, loading up the rattlebox Commercial again and heading back into the night.

It was on nights like these that I would leave the stage and go down the hall to listen to the band.

When they played instrumentals or when Billy sang at the mike with the saxophone hanging loosely around his middle, Jaysus, it was a real turn on.

As well as Billy, David on drums, Damien on guitar and Torry on bass, all sang, and, in their own styles did a decent job of it. But again in the vocal arena, as in every other, Brown was something special. I used to wonder why they needed a singer at all. There was no shortage of them and Sean Mahon hadn't even started yet. I suspected that here was a dark horse in the vocal stakes, but no matter how hard the lads would encourage it the dark-featured trombonist would have none of it.

Back to Billy Brown. When he sang he had a natural feel with which only the chosen few are gifted. The quality of his voice would win him fans all over the globe and it would have a seductive effect in any era, but in those early days of the 1960s it was a real treat to hear a master at work. There didn't seem to be a discipline at which this mysterious man couldn't excel. And it was no bother to him, no bullshit or tantrums involved in all this great unexpressed and unacclaimed talent. All that would come later.

The only time there were any ripples of unrest in the brethren would be at rehearsals in Ballymena, when Bill would regularly turn up later than the rest of us. He lived in Larne, and David and I lived in Belfast and Mahon drove from Downpatrick. Bill had the farthest to travel and we were not far behind. We would all assemble in the Flamingo Ballroom at the anointed hour and exchange small talk as we, typically, waited for Bill to appear.

"Where the fuck have you been and what sort of

time is this to come at?" Maurice would rage, with veins standing out in his neck.

"Hiya men," he would reply nonchalantly before addressing the boss. "I got stuck on the Hill trying to help a farmer pull his sheep out of the snow." He'd smile and look straight into his enraged leader's eyes.

There would be no snow outside in Ballymena; indeed it might not even be winter, but that would not deter the master excuse-maker.

"You can't see it here, of course, but Shane's Hill is impassable. Barely made it myself."

"And that's not lemonade I smell on you," Maurice would counter. "This shit is just not good enough."

At this juncture Billy's amazing stammer would surface. He had this amazing ability to work the lips, without intelligible sound, as his brain searched for the proper face-saving response.

And when it came, it would end the dispute. Something along the lines of: "Oh well, we better get down to business, it's getting on."

And that would be that. The band would begin listening to the latest chart-topper that we had determined we should do, and Billy would get down to the biz of giving out parts. The rhythm section and lead guitar would invariably work out their own bits, but the brass men needed an arranger. Who else but Bill? He would tell Maurice what notes to blow and he would blow his own horn alongside and then he would give the trombone part to Sean and the same ritual would continue until the song had been completed and the horns were tight. You had to know what tight was to play tight, but it made all the difference when the gig was on and war had been declared.

I would sing it a couple of times and if there was any harmony involved, then the latecomer would arrange these lines as well. Nothing more would be said about the row and we would work until about eleven and then over to the Wee Keg bar across the road and on home.

Why anyone would be gasping for a drink at that time of night was beyond my understanding in those days. A good feed was more like it in my book. I was a complete teetotaller and was still honouring a pledge I had taken at Confirmation not to drink until I reached the age of 21. I was in no way a religious lad, but there seemed to be a great deal of sense about this particular abstention. The abiding image of alcohol in my head was of three things: blood, vomiting and fighting. And who in under Jaysus would want any of that? No way, far better to get a charge of chips and, if the funds stretched, maybe a pork pie or a piece of fish.

Davy McKnight and myself would head back to the city in his battered old Hillman, with it smelling like a chipper. The banter was always about women and music. I would be dropped off at the college campus; a ring of the front doorbell was needed to get a lad in, and as long as you were sober and alone, you could expect to escape the report card.

I should mention here something really weird about the learning process concerning songs. It was always the same and I have never been able to work it out. It happened with all the brethren.

At rehearsal, Damien would produce a disc with the word that this was a chart-breaker and we should get onto it immediately. Unless the thing was an absolute stinker, we would readily agree, because this was one of the guitarist's many talents; his ability to identify hits in advance of them actually charting. So after "learning" the ditty as I've already outlined, we would run over it a couple of times before finishing for the night. We rehearsed until we knew it backwards.

At the next gig, however, when Maurice would call the number, panic would ensue. This would happen even after listening to it on the cassette player en route to the gig.

"Ah fuck it, Maurice, leave it and we'll have a run at it afterwards," would be the cry, but to no avail. The bossman would insist that we do the thing and he'd instruct Davy on drums to count it in. It was always wise to have a copy of the words at your feet on the floor as a cue-sheet, but that was of little help in the fog of deafness that would unavoidably follow. Not only would the singing be extremely dodgy, but the instrumentals would also be sometimes found, shall we say, wanting. Laughter was a great cure-all, but out-and-out hysteria was frowned upon by Maurice.

And then, the wonder of it all. Having made a complete balls of the work first time around, we would do the same song before the end note-perfect and it would be thus for as long as it remained in the programme. And that happened every time we played a new song. In the scheme of all great things, this is hardly a mind boggler, but it was a strange one nevertheless. Whatever the routine at rehearsals, the thing sounded wonderful live on stage and that was what mattered. It was going well.

Six

Borris-in-Ossory Wake-up Call

We were building a reputation all over the North and the prognosis seemed good. We had graduated to gold lamé suits, which we would wear for the second half of the show, and the fans seemed to approve. These were the days of tight trousers and the rolled-up newspaper stuffed down one leg to impress the ladies and maybe some of the lads. I never actually got round to that, as the serpent was more than capable of holding his own with the paper prosthetics. By that I mean he was always in constant movement. Any irregular motion at all would guarantee that he'd be up for inspection as to possible targets.

Maurice was doing a passable job with the bookings and there was still no sign of our big "breakthrough" into the South. Then one night we were rehearsing in the Flamingo and he got a phone call from, as Sammy shouted up to the bandstand, "The Free State".

He came back rubbing his hands, proclaiming we had finally managed to get a date in the Holy Land. We had a booking in Borris-in-Ossory. None of us had ever heard of it before, but that didn't matter. We were going to play in front of Southerners and we celebrated doubly when he added that, after expenses, we could expect a pay night of eight pounds apiece. It was a nine–one Sunday-night gig and it would mean us leaving Ballymena at about one in the afternoon, but that wasn't even discussed. We were on our way to the big time. Wait until they heard what we had in store for them. There was this idea that, once we had an introduction to the Southern dancers, word would spread like it was doing in the North and it would then be only a matter of time until we were robbing all the orchards of our choice.

The Saturday night before the Southern gig we were in Coleraine in the Boathouse and, with the programme we had at the time, the reception was hot. We played a fair share of chart-toppers of the day and also featured some stuff that Damien and the lads had decided would appeal to the fair crowd of non-chart-based music fans who followed us from venue to venue. We would be into stuff that was barely popular in the States, and there was a definite crowd who loved to hear just that ... a fan base. Truth is, there was a growing band of young people who were starved of anything other than "Sugar Sugar". These kids wanted a bit of "Vinegar Vinegar" and we were the boys to do it. There was no definite musical plan; nobody was preaching a brand of music. We all had a little competition within the band when it came to writing our own songs. Sometimes we would talk about recording one of our own tunes, but there was never an orchestrated discussion along the lines of, "OK then, let's hear them all. Let's see what we have to offer and we will pick the best two and stick them out." It was always assumed that we would record originals when the time was right, but there was no structure, no auditions, so to speak. Most of the Freshmen were into writing their own stuff, but we had no forum within the band, either to decide on a style, or even initiate a plan to develop one. We were too busy aping other people's and enjoying the fruits of their labour.

Off we set for Borris-in-Ossory in County Laois and, as we headed out in the Morris, there was a real sense of anticipation. Mainly, what would the women be like? Would they be as horny as their Northern cousins and would the band score direct hits when the music was done? In no time at all the six or seven hours flew in and seven Ulster raiders descended upon the small hamlet of B-in-O, barely making it in time for the welcome fry that the promoter had arranged for us before the off.

We humped the gear in first before sitting down to the grub, and it didn't take long to disappear. Setting up was fairly simple and we changed into our brown suits for the first half of the gig.

It was strange listening to the accents of the locals who were really friendly and I'm sure they, in turn, had never heard the mixture of accents coming at them from the hungry horde of Northern musos.

It can be difficult enough sometimes to make out the wonderful inflexions and tones of the County Antrim dialect.

For the first hour or so things were fairly normal. Men and women came into the hall and sat down along the sides, or ambled along to the mineral and tea bar and surveyed the scene. The culture of the time ordained that it was the women who were first into the ballroom and they would naturally inspect the stage, just as naturally as you would inspect them. They were first into the halls because, as already noted, it was deemed unladylike for them to drink in pubs. Only "loose" women, God bless 'em, would be seen in the bars of the day.

There was rarely much action before half ten at most gigs on a Sunday night, as pub closing at the time was ten o'clock. And sure enough, around that time, there was a definite change in the tempo and heat of the evening, when the men sauntered into the hall to a chorus of "yahoos" and "yaboyas" as they made their grand entrance, suitably prepared for the night ahead. They didn't seem to be taking too much notice of what was happening up on the stand and, with nobody dancing, it was with a degree of relief that we left the stage at eleven o'clock and featured our three-quarter inch tape recorder, which was to provide the music whilst we transformed ourselves into the rockin' superstars we imagined ourselves to be. In other words, we were dying a death, but I imagined that when we came back wearing the gold lamé suits we would still win the night.

There was no dressing room and we stood behind a curtain – seven men bumping into each other and cursing as we changed. There was also, as I recall, some laughter, but it was more of a cry of disbelief at what was happening outside. If you ever try it, you will quickly discover that there is no way of just walking onto a stage in front of an audience wearing a glitzy gold, ball-squeezing suit. There has to be attitude. Big attitude. You have to bounce, if you like, or better still jump; but there's no way you can casually stroll on. But to do it seven times, from behind a curtain, was asking a bit much, so it was decided that the lads would go on ahead and leave the leppin' to me. The show must go on and all that, but there was a definite touch of embarrassment involved in going back out to a disinterested crowd dressed like a shimmering spaceman.

The opening bars of something or other were belting out as I pranced onto the stage and gave it all I could muster. It felt like I was trying to set off fireworks at a funeral, but there was no holding back.

Here you have it folks, this is it – this is what you've been waiting to hear. This is the renewal of the feast of Babylon, the new Annunciation; this is Gabriel blowing his horn with a hard-on. Men, keep your cock in your trousers, and ladies, don't throw off your knickers just yet; there's more and better coming.

I tried every trick I knew and the band blew so hard you could nearly touch the blue electric light coming from the horns. I desperately tried to pick up on a friendly face, a lady in waiting, or a grinning farmer, but there was nothing; nobody was interested or so it seemed. But I didn't stop rocking. It was way beyond my control. I was away in the head and wouldn't stop until the hot contact kundalini energy line, which linked my brain to the serpent and proceeded down to my feet and then back up into my spine before starting all over again, had been broken by the drum crescendo and Brown tonguing a "shut up, Bigman, this is the final word" riff, from the bell on the hottest sax south of the Lagan.

Silence.

There was nothing to do but continue and, as we were halfway through the second song, the promoter came over to the side of the stage. The chap could see that we were breaking our balls trying to get the party started and he had a sympathetic look on his face as he whispered into Maurice's ear.

"OK, lads; they want an old-time waltz and they'll dance."

It was as simple as that. Just stop the jumpin' and cavortin' about and give them what they wanted to hear. We didn't have an old-time waltz in the repertoire. We had never been asked to play one before, but if it was deemed to be some sort of a starting mechanism to get this crowd going, then sure we could pull a few out of the fire.

Off went Davy on the drums – oom cha cha, oom cha cha – and Bill blew a waltz on the sax. Sure enough, the floor was black within a couple of bars and as the rest of the band joined in, we were consoled to see that at least the wake was over.

We all had a waltz to sing, and I rendered "The Boys from the County Armagh". But I felt a right eejit singing it wearing a gold lamé suit.

One o'clock finally arrived and there was a great sense of relief the bastard gig was over. No man was sad. There was no action. No frenzy, no sweat. We got polite applause and looked and felt like eejits and, needless to say, we didn't even bother to hand out our photos. What a bummer. No women and, truth to tell, nobody was in any form to face one. I think that we all imagined we heard the dream being shattered at different times during that evening. As we loaded the van up for the several-hour trip back to Ballymena and Belfast, there was too much disillusionment among the brethren to raise much talk about anything. Just get the hell out of Borris-in-Ossory.

The thought that we had played to people who had a different set of expectations of a night out, of the music they liked, and of the volume they liked to hear it played at, was a right come-down to Reality Row and a real wake-up call. We all had a belief that we were, somehow, going to have the same reception in darkest Laois as we got in the North. But they hadn't taken to us, or our music. We had failed. This was a first, and being ignored was hard to take. The egos were badly bruised that night by the cold, silent hands of B-in-O and, by extension, our journey into the much-anticipated centres of the Free State such as Dublin, Cork, Galway and Limerick, now seemed a lifetime away. It was a strange run home; sat in the same place for too many bumpy hours, setting out in darkness but getting bright by the time we reached the border. We paid our "late crossing tax" to the customs man on duty and shuffled on. It was hard to raise a laugh, but we eventually saw the funny side of it and the eight quid in the pocket wasn't to be sneezed at either. There was a lot of time to spend and, not for the last time, the journey home seemed to take an eternity. It was like rolling along in a smoke-filled coffin. All the windows were shut against the night and those who could slept, while the rest shifted positions as best as possible to allow much-needed blood to flow to the cheeks of bony rumps.

There's no business like showbusiness.

Needless to say, there was no great urge to repeat the Borris experience amongst the lads, and when we did our next gig in the North in Portrush, things returned to normal. Service as usual.

Make the music, raise the temperature, sing the joy and try to get laid. It was hidden somewhere in the back of my mind that we would have to select the Southern gigs with more emphasis on the cities, as in talking to some of the other Northern bands, like the Plattermen and Glover we found that they had the same experience. Dublin was to become the target. That would be our route to the big time.

By now there was regular talk of getting a manager, but there was more discussion of going "full-time". The burden of two jobs, one paying considerably less than the other, meant that very soon the "day job" would be gone. Questions were asked of me: would I throw in the studying and join the professional ranks? There was no doubt in my mind: who in their right mind would refuse such an offer? I was completely addicted to the music these men made and full of wonder and awe at the talents of the Brown brother. He made the place light up when he played the saxophone and clarinet. He didn't use a keyboard in those days, only whatever piano would be onstage at the gigs. Most were too battered by abuse over the years. They couldn't be amplified properly, anyway, and sticking a Shure head into the uplifted lid was a bit hit and miss. He had no keyboard because they weren't yet available and any that were couldn't take the hammering they would get, not only from a fast-handed pusher, but also in the back of a van, being driven home to Ballymena by a tired Von Fangio type who thought he was still on the Formula One circuit.

But going full-time pro was my dream. I didn't foresee the problems that would arise when I tried to fulfil it. My contract with the college was unknown to me. I had passed certain exams and, as a result, chose to go to St Joseph's Training College for young Catholic teachers. It wasn't really a choice. I could have gone to Queen's University in Belfast, but as my old college buddy Michael was already at the "Ranch", as the teacher's indoctrination centre was fondly known, the choice was a simple one.

He had assured me that I would need to be really stupid not to coast the course and guaranteed that no serious thinking or work would ever be contemplated. This suited me fine. Queen's, on the other hand, held the threat of more genuine study and would require a certain amount of effort. My only ambition was to sing, so a few years dossing on the teacher-training front fell in nicely with whatever plans I had.

One night on the way home from a gig, as Maurice was splitting the cash, the decision was made.

"OK lads, we all hand in our notice and in two weeks' time, we either sink or swim," was the gist of it and there was a sense of commitment I had never experienced before. This was it; this was the move that would take me to Heaven, and when we were fully professional the accompanying status would set us further along the road to fame and fortune.

It was my dream coming true and something I'd imagined since I'd started imagining. There was a sense of satisfaction with this move into full-time ranks, and it had always been my destiny. Jaysus, it was the only place to be.

"Sorry, Mr McMenamin, we can't agree to that proposal, and if you leave the college, you or your family will have to pay back to HM government the cost of your education here to date, along with any grant monies you have received. Now, if you had completed three years of the four-year course, we would allow you to leave and give you a teacher's certificate at the same time."

Death sentence. This was the complete nightmare. The course had become a curse. Pay back from what? Every shilling I made in the band was absent without permission. They say money talks, and it's probably true. However, the word it kept repeating to me was "goodbye". I knew a lot of guys in Strabane like that. If you had it, you spent it or gave it away. Maybe you gave it as a loan, but it was never really expected back. And back it never came. I knew without asking that there was no chance of such money being available to repay Mrs Windsor's educational agents in Ulster and when I explained my dilemma to the Freshmen, there was a deafening silence.

"You're the man, Bigman, but you're not that much of a big man," was the general feeling, and it was made clear that, with or without me, the other lads were going ahead.

No one even exhorted me to get a loan to meet the commitment to the Northern Ireland educational system, as everyone understood it was impossible. In the early 1960s, such things didn't happen and the amount of dosh required was way beyond us all. In any case, I had come to understand the system of fiscal governance, simply known as "Bob Down, Rubber Knocker". It had come to popularity with the advent of credit, especially that available from the many travelling salesmen who would knock on your door in the evening time selling their wares, firstly from a suitcase on the back of a bicycle and later from a car. These Oriental gentlemen sprang up along the Northwest and would be most adept at convincing housewives of the worthiness of their brushes or trousers or whatever was in their Pandora's box. Nylons, knickers and shirts would be offloaded for the mere deposit of, say, a shilling. Then, forthwith, the heavy door knocker would be exchanged for a rubber one and thus when Mr Bawalpaindi came a-knocking a week later, he couldn't be heard and so could be ignored. I do believe this arrangement was very popular all over the North at the time, but the sellers made enough lolly to keep themselves in business and everyone happy.

I never imagined the unseen mandarins of the Northern Ireland civil service would entertain this radical approach to financial problem-solving so, as they say, Aughrim was truly lost.

Sounds pathetic when I look back, but at the time it was a monstrous threat. "If you don't reimburse the Exchequer for the money wasted on you, then the might of HMG will be brought to bear on your big warbling head." It seemed like my career would end before it really began.

The pain of it all was brought home when we did a gig in Strabane's dancehall, the Pallidrome, a few nights later.

"You might as well call it a day after the gig," said Maurice as we travelled over the Glenshane Pass en route to the home of the Clippers. "We can drop you off at your place on the way back." It was a Friday and I'll never, ever, forget the sense of doom as we hacked the gear into the big, cold, empty tomb. There were still no relief bands to play for the first few hours, so it was a five-hour torture. It was a weird, desolate, desperate feeling as I sang my songs in a daze. Here I was in my home town, singing at my own wake. The women drifted in, as usual, and the men came later, having completed the required ritual of taking a few drinks to muster up the courage of taking to the floor with their potential victims.

I knew most of the audience by name and there was no sense of occasion whatsoever. There was definitely no blue light coming from me and, as usual at home-town gigs, the crowd made no attempt to clap "one of their own". It was a given that if you dared stand up in front of them you had the necessary talent to do so, and therefore no applause was required. It would have been extra hard to impress these people anyway. After all, Strabane and its sons had started the whole showband thing with the Clipper Carlton and you wouldn't expect anything other than the best from a local. The Clippers had set the bar very high.

Actually, I couldn't sing for the last half hour of the gig and the band played on. Christ Jesus's agony on the cross was repeated within my soul. This was despair alright, and a sense of self-hate and loathing was my emotional response to the infectious rhythms and sounds emanating from my soon-to-be-departed mates. They weren't going to die, of course; it was just me who was in for that fate. They were moving on. And here I was, the eunuch of the Freshmen; the man without the balls to tell whoever needed telling to fuck off and leave a young man at peace with his dreams.

Unlike Jesus, there was no sense of sacrifice, which could have made the gig a bit more palatable. I was leaving this living joy because of fear, primarily fear that I would be in all kinds of brown stuff if I didn't pay back the money. It was impossible to do a "rubber knocker job" on the government, as they had all sorts of angles with which to threaten impoverishment. They controlled the benefits which accrued to most homes in the Northwest and, anyway, the crowd that controlled the purse strings wouldn't have had much sympathy with a big Taig who was turning his back on education in favour of the frivolous pursuit of music as a career. This was the early 1960s when everything in the North closed down on a Sunday, including the public parks. So if you couldn't walk the oul mutt on a certain day because of the risk of offending a righteous Creator, then getting a hard-on in a pleasure palace of a dancehall instead of teaching was not even a starter.

"There you go, Bigman," said Maurice as he pulled the small van to a stop outside my parents' rented home in Bridge Street.

I had taken my leave of the lads individually after the scourging in the hall and all that was left was to evacuate the hellhole in the Morris Commercial and open the hall door. There were no tears, but the lump in my throat stopped me from saying anything at all.

For the first time in my life I hugged men. Davy the drummer, Sean and Billy, looked sad at my departing, but no other emotion was shown. Condolences were uttered after the gig, but it was a silent van as I stepped out.

And they were gone. "What a fuckin' loser", or words to that effect pierced my heart as I opened the hall door, reeking with self-pity and not fit company even for myself. The old house on the Bridgend used to be infested with cockroaches, and I vehemently crushed them on the lino floor as I sat down and firmly believed that my life had ended just then and that I would never be able to become involved with a group of guys like this ever again.

What conversation, if any, continued in the van after my departure I have no idea, but knowing them it was probably along the lines of: "Fuck him, we are heading to the top anyway".

There was no sleep for me that night. I was a waking dead man. The spirit would never rise again, I was banjaxed.

SEVEN

The Student Corpse

The next year at the teachers' training college in Belfast was a daily grind. The band I had started there had long disappeared from the scene and when I tried to revive it, it just never seemed to work out. The atmosphere at rehearsals was non-existent, and soon it became apparent there was to be no going back. We just couldn't get it to happen and it petered out. Not with a bang, but a with whimper as the man says.

The curriculum for the third year in teachers' training was a bit of a doddle. We mostly spent our spare time playing poker in our various lodgings and at night we would head into Belfast city centre to try and find a bit of devilment. It was during this time that I got to hear some of the bands on the circuit and one that really knocked me out was Johnny Flynn; in particular his drummer, the late Frankie (Flash)

Hannon. It was hard to make out which was the more infectious, his drumming or his smile. I watched his antics one night for the entire performance and as he rested his ear over the snare drum, a wicked smile would create lines of light all over the kit. He came, like the rest of the band, from Tuam in County Galway, but his drumming was from somewhere west of the river Bann – somewhere like Strabane.

And, of course, there was the Royal Showband, featuring Brendan Bowyer. I got to hear him play in Belfast one night, and knew that the next time they came back the joint would be stuffed. Boyer had a magic about him that had Irish audiences enthralled. His voice was superb on big ballads and his style inspired many imitators in the years that followed. The man sang from his soul and his wailing touched the sincerity nerve in every woman's heart. And, as I said earlier, where the women flocked, the men would surely follow. The rest of the outfit were cheery chappies, but they hardly set the place alight. Boyer was the man, and with him onstage there wasn't much need for anything else.

The Freshmen had decided to change their name to Six of One. They went off to England to tour the Mecca circuit and played in all the major ballrooms across the UK. They had the talent, of course, to manage without a lead singer, as they were all fairly handy at the microphone and the presence of Master Brown filled all gaps.

They recorded a song by Charlie and Inez Fox. "He's The One You Love" was well received in Ireland after their return, but they decided to give up on the six-piece concept and employ a frontman again.

I would scour the weekend papers to see if there was any mention of them and soon discovered that they had a new man fronting the band by the name of Tommy Drennan. He was a tenor from Limerick city and, by all accounts, from what I was reading, he had a trained voice, which was destined to take the country by storm. Jaysus, I felt bad. I was secretly praying that he'd slip on a giant banana skin, but that was just me being pathetic. I was envious, jealous, pissed off and any other defective state you can imagine.

I used to get that "big empty hole in the belly feeling" when I heard their name mentioned. I remember one night going to a dance in Omagh to listen to the Plattermen and afterwards I spoke to their leader, Pat Chesters – no mean saxophonist himself. We spoke about Billy Brown and how talented a lad he was. He had often come along to hear the band, well, to hear Bill, when the band played locally. When I was leaving he said, "You never know, Bigman; it might all work out yet." I think I laughed at the very idea.

By now it was 1963 and the Freshmen were a regular feature in the Belfast papers. Things seemed to be going well for them and the regret in my head wasn't getting any easier to live with.

It was around this time that I had two offers to join new outfits that were starting up as a result of splits in existing bands. One offer to come knocking on my door in Belfast was from the New Clippers. Some of the original members were stood around the lounge of my lodgings in Andersonstown one morning as I was summoned from the cot to speak with legends I had grown up adoring. The unannounced arrival of these great superstars of my youth left me speechless and I was very impressed and honoured that they had bothered to ask me to enlist for the cause, but it was the same old story. Their first gig was a month-long booking in Scotland and, besides, I had been approached a few days earlier by an old mate, Henry McCullough, to join him in a new band he was starting in Enniskillen. This was going to be a semi-pro venture and that seemed like a decent way to get back into the music.

But after just one rehearsal with Henry's band, the miracle happened.

I was doing teaching practice in Strabane when I heard that the Freshmen had parted company with Tommy Drennan. The banana skin had materialised.

I forget how I heard the news, but when Davy McKnight rang me that day at the school where I taught, I couldn't believe my luck. There was a chance that I might be considered for the job again, but I would need to be fully committed to the cause and, if asked, join immediately.

I jumped. Fuck college, to hell with exams, screw the NI educational system. This was my second chance; the end of the nightmare and the beginning of the adventure. No stopping this time; there would be no turning back.

I travelled to a gig in Belfast to see the band and was delighted with the reception they got from the crowd and the greeting I received from them. It was agreed.

This time Maurice took me aside and explained, with sound Ballymena financial reasoning, that as they had worked for over a year building up their reputation without me, it would be unreasonable on my part to expect an equal share in the divvy-up of the money. He was talking to a man in a dream. Had he asked me to work for nothing for a year, I'd have agreed. The intricate monetary plan he had deemed as fair was lost on me. It didn't matter, it wasn't important; I was the High King of All Ireland. I really felt I was the man.

When I told St Joseph's Training College that I was heading for the hills, they amazed me with their response: "Come back in a few months and do your exams and, all being well, we will award you your teacher's certificate." They explained that it would be a shame to miss out on it, seeing as how I'd completed my teaching practice and seemed to be near enough the finished article.

What a surprise. It worked out perfectly. The band was working all over the North as usual, so there would be no problem fitting them in. I wasn't worried about sitting the tests; as I mentioned earlier, a person would need to be really absent upstairs to fail them.

The day the exams ended was a night off from the band and a poker school in the digs was arranged for the afternoon before the school hols. My life was sunny in the extreme, but that afternoon a darkness fell which was unimaginable in its horrific tragedy and which would have a profound effect on my young heart. It certainly broke it into tiny pieces.

The *craic* was good during the poker school and there was an air of relief and celebration that the exams were over and, apparently, all hands had done reasonably well. I lived with a young Belfast couple, Tony and Rita Jordan, who were buying their first home and having a couple of students to help out financially made life a little easier. The house was in Andersonstown, which was handy for the college. Tony and Rita were a very happy couple and the focus of their joy was their little infant son of thirteen months, Eddie. He had just been born when I first moved in with them and he was a right little star.

The Jordans were real Belfast friendly, married for a short while and very much in love. They exhibited that certain Northern black humour on a daily basis, were very generous people and they loved the *craic* from a couple of demented students; one from Strabane and the other out of Derry.

Rita was a blonde looker and was totally natural with us all. Jaysus, she wasn't much older than us, so there was never any sense of inconvenience, any sense of "well you're here and we're glad of your money, but would prefer it if you weren't" sort of thing. She smiled and laughed a lot. She was a delightful presence and I always thought that Tony was a very lucky man.

As we settled down early in the afternoon for a few hands of poker, little did we know of the tragedy about to enter the front door and change all our lives forever.

The school was proceeding with no great adventure when a caller came to visit Tony, who was out at his work as a plumber-fitter. He was an old mate from the Shankill area of the city, a fact that was strange enough in itself, but this was long before the war that would blight the area in about ten years hence. Not too many people crossed the religious divide, even in those comparatively peaceful days.

This man called because he had some work he

thought Tony could do and wished to speak to him about it. It was explained that Tony wasn't at home but should be home shortly and that he could wait if he wanted.

"Can I have a game, lads?" said he.

"If you have the dough, you're in," was the macho reply.

There were four players from the college and this newcomer made it five. As he was about to sit down, the stranger produced two automatic pistols, which he introduced with a jokey, "Well now boys, there'll be no cheating in this house."

There was no objection at that point. We looked on in absolute awe at the guns. These were the Real McCoy and each one of us did what all young men do when they see a gun for the first time; we pointed it and went "boom".

We played excitedly with the guns for about twenty minutes. I inspected both and felt a sense of power in the very act of holding them.

Our gun-toting visitor then took the weapons back from us and, with a great show of bravado, produced a clip of ammunition, which he hammered into the handle of one of them, the Luger. This was like the stuff you would have seen with Edward G. Robinson or John Wayne in the movies or something, but when the gun was loaded, all hands dissented.

"Aw for fuck's sake, you can't do that, leave it out," was the general chorus of disapproval from us as he placed the loaded weapon on top of the table that we were using for the cards. One of the lads lifted the gun and gingerly placed it on top of the cabinet beside us. A sense of fear and awareness had replaced that of wonder once the ammunition had been produced.

It's difficult to recall the exact train of events that followed, but the horror that resulted is all too vivid in my mind's eye.

Rita was working in the kitchen and the baby was just toddling about and looking for attention the way all normal young kids do.

"Sambos lads," was the welcome call from the other room and we trooped in to sample Rita's famous Belfast doorsteps. She made great food and we all sat around the table, chewing and chomping and talking about nothing in particular. Little Eddie was bouncing up and down on my knee and as one of the students left the table to go back into the lounge, the little guy toddled down and followed him.

A few seconds later, little Eddie Jordan was shot through the head just below his tiny nose. The stupefied shooter had pointed the loaded gun at him as he waddled into the lounge and, forgetting that the killing thing was loaded, aimed it at the little boy and pulled the trigger.

It was a tragic accident, which to this day defies explanation. I was standing just behind the child and was shocked at the noise of the gun being fired. As I looked on in absolute bewilderment, another bullet grazed my nose. The gun had a hair-trigger, which meant that if you even touched it the thing would unleash its deadly venom again. The horrified student holding the spitting weapon was frozen to the spot and his face had turned green. Maybe shock played tricks with my eyes, but I can still see his contorted face: full of terror but definitely green.

Little Eddie swayed for an unforgettable moment and before he collapsed onto the carpet, the man who had brought the guns into the house swept him up and ran to his car in a frantic dash to the Royal Victoria Hospital.

Screaming. Pandemonium. Terror. Disbelief. Despair.

To the day I die, I shall never forget the heart-rending wail that followed. And for the first time in my life, I experienced tragedy.

Rita was hysterical in the kitchen and as she was about seven months pregnant with her second child, I ran back to slap her face. It was all I could think of doing, but I had seen it done before and was afraid she would lose her unborn child if something drastic wasn't done. She stopped screaming and her trembling voice asked if her little boy was safe. I was operating on some sort of emergency system and don't quite remember what I said, but I know I told her a lie. I assured her that Eddie was only grazed and was safe in hospital.

Then I took flight. There was no phone in the house and I sprinted up to the phone box just up the hill and pulled a man out who was using it. I was screaming something or other and somehow managed to make the 999 call. I didn't know who I was calling, what service or what I wanted to do. I think I asked for an ambulance, a doctor and a priest.

Running away from the phone, I headed off down the Andersonstown Road, past Casement Park and on down the Falls Road. The thought was somewhere in the back of my mind that I was running to the hospital to see Eddie, and that this damnation really hadn't happened at all. If I could get there quick enough, then all would be OK. I ran and ran and ran and ran. It seemed as if my legs had wings attached. I was flying. I was driven. I know now that I was trying to run away from the horror of it all.

When I reached the turn-off for the hospital, I couldn't stop my relentless retreat from reality. I finally reached another phone box in North Queen Street – if you know Belfast, then you'll appreciate that it's a fair way from Andersonstown to Queen Street – and I was barely able to catch my breath. Panic-driven and heart pounding with shock, this time I managed to call the hospital.

Eddie was pronounced dead on arrival at the Royal Victoria and the message to me was to "contact the police, they are looking for you".

Back in the death house, the doctor had arrived and was attempting to sedate Rita. I ended up at Andersonstown Barracks and it was in a daze that I recall Tony entering to see us.

He had returned from work as normal and got the fright of his life to see the large crowd assembled outside the house. His poor mind thought that something terrible had happened to Rita and when he discovered that it was Eddie, it was with a "sense of near relief" that he uncovered the truth. There was no comfort, of course, for the ravaged couple.

Words cannot adequately describe the demonic nature of that afternoon. The next few days are a blur now, as they were at the time, but I recall sitting beside Tony in the black funeral limo and him trying to open the tiny white coffin that held his darling son.

He was beside himself with grief. He had been afforded no chance of taking his farewell of his boy.

He had gone off to work as usual and was never to lay eyes on Eddie again. It was agonising to watch him rest the white coffin on his lap and mind-numbing to dissuade him from opening it.

Tony doesn't stand much more than five and a half feet tall, but himself and his wife showed the strength and stature of giants. They consoled the shooter. They testified at the subsequent trial that the whole thing was a tragedy, an accident, and a terrible affliction; there was no bitterness in their testimony. They stuck together, and Rita, overcoming her terrific grief, gave birth to a daughter a few months later.

I recall how, after the burial of their baby son, they drove off together in their car. I thought someone should go with them to give a bit of comfort and solace, but the Dean of Trench House, Fr Donal McEnaney, assured me that it was best to leave them alone and let them begin the healing process. Mac, as he was known, was a loving and wise man. He was a tower of strength to all during those darkest of days.

The man who brought the guns into the blighted house denied ownership. He testified that he had found them in the boot of a car that he had recently bought. He assured all and sundry that they had been hidden in the spare wheel and he had only discovered them that very afternoon.

But I believe we were all to blame. We all handled the guns and aimed them at each other. They were blank of course, but then again we always imagine they are. The lesson learned was that you should never point a gun unless you intend to kill something or someone.

The very next day after the funeral, I travelled to

a gig with the band in Portrush in County Antrim. Amazingly, I went onstage and sang my big head off. There was no reaction to the tragedy. I seemed to be operating on autopilot. Whatever about going back to work if your job was as a teacher, say, or a carpenter, it seemed very inappropriate to go back to singing. Life goes on for sure and that's the way it has to be, but I was feeling guilty about doing this as it seemed like I was letting Tony and Rita down.

There was a sense of frivolity about the whole band business, but it wasn't strong enough to deter me from getting up there and doing it. There was a certain feeling of unreality about the music; singing songs, showboating and dressing up. It was as if I had been filleted on the inside and what was on show was merely a shell, a performing shell but nonetheless an empty one.

I never mentioned any of this to the brethren and they, in turn, didn't make too big a fuss over me. I just continued on as per normal, and everything seemed to be the same as always. But things came to a head on a Saturday night in the Floral Hall, a great big cavernous mausoleum on the outskirts of Belfast.

It was about three weeks after the fatal event and it was the first time the band had managed to get a gig there. There was a resident band playing before us and by now our stage entrance had evolved into a fairly slick, one-man-at-a-time production. Very few dancehalls had a curtained stage and in an attempt to compensate for this and to build up a bit of an atmosphere, we had devised this start to the show.

Davy would walk onto the empty stage and begin drumming. He'd lay down a feverish teen beat and then Torry would come on and start up on the bass

guitar and so on until the whole band was belting
out an intro and building the excitement with a fairly
hectic repetitive riff. I would then wait until I could
feel the buzz and then run on, throw a few shapes
and inject some vocal excitement, with a few buck
leps into the proceedings.

But the boys were wailing away and, try as I
might, I couldn't move. I was frozen to the spot; my
brain was telling me to run on, but I couldn't budge.
The sound of the rhythm disappeared and my brow
began to sweat. A couple of the lads were nodding
me out and when they looked into the wings, I burst
into tears. Big salty rivers of tears ran down my
cheeks and into my mouth.

Jaysus, I couldn't stop. Delayed reaction, post-
traumatic collapse, is what it would be called today.
But back then in 1963, I just thought I was bollixed.
Damien McIlroy stepped up to the mike and did the
business. The rest of the night is a blur, but I know
I didn't sing; it was impossible. I felt like giving the
whole thing up.

The feeling persisted that somehow we were
all to blame for letting the guy into the poker game
and that life would never be the same again. The
scene played out, again and again, in my head. The
excitement of the guns and the big macho feeling
of holding a real shooter in my hand. What a fool I
had been. I was never able to discuss the anguish; its
tragedy was too hurtful, this crime for which nobody
paid. It was a slow-burning misery which brought
me back to the college to Mac and which led to his
suggestion that I go back to Tony and his lovely wife
Rita, and apologise to them.

"Let them know how sorry you are, Derek, and

you will help yourself by trying to help them." I did it. I met with Tony and we talked a lot about the tragic events and how it would be possible to continue with all our lives. I wasn't looking for absolution; the fact that someone else had pulled the trigger was scant comfort. I don't really know what I was looking for, but what Mac had said was valid. I was more concerned with trying to console this bereaved, blameless man and his wife than I was with my own pathetic state, whatever that was. I told him that I would have done anything to replay that desperate day, to start it again.

And, as Mac had predicted, though I will never forget the whole dreadful affair, that was the beginning of my healing. The wound still weeps from time to time and I hope that writing this part of my Freshmen story will help tell a little of Eddie's story.

A friend of mine, Brian Maguire, a man who spends his life painting powerful, unbeautiful art, told me that he had spent nearly five years reading up on victims of the Second World War. He read countless books and studied endless papers and one thing, above all else, was apparent to him. Every victim demanded that his or her story be told. When I thought about this, I decided he was one hundred per cent right.

If the story of their wasted lives wasn't made known, then they would remain forever just that; lost, darkened spirits whose light would never shine. No one can ever make up for the future that was taken away that day from Tony and Rita's little man. But one thing is for certain.

He was the innocent victim.

EIGHT

Things Get Better

Things were really starting to happen for the band. We spoke about getting a manager and, sure enough, one appeared from the side of one of the ballrooms. The great Peter Dempsey introduced himself to us one night after a gig and he got the job. I noticed him standing in the same spot without moving all night and thought that this wasn't the first time I'd seen him. He was a Belfast man and had the same idea as ourselves, namely that we were heading somewhere good and that he wanted a slice of the action. "I am the man to make this band happen and I have the contacts to do it," said he and we willingly believed him.

The Van from Hell, the old battered Morris, had been replaced by a big pleasure palace that featured individual airline-type seats, each with its own headrest and antimacassar. I think it sat about 14 in comfort and speed, and there was even an aisle down which a man could walk before he settled down for the journey. This was some luxury.

Whatever "Bob Down, Rubber Knocker" system Maurice and the lads were employing, it worked, and the Freshmen van paraded proudly throughout the North and also, by now, to lots of smaller towns down below. It was fitted with a super-duper, whooper-pooper, powered engine that allowed us to shatter all speed records then existing in the six counties. Fitted wardrobes at the back meant that we could now separate the wearing gear from the working gear and instruments and cases had their own dedicated space in front of the big double doors at the back. Painted here and down both sides beneath the windows was the name: "Freshmen, Ballymena". Why it was deemed necessary to stick an identity tag on the origin of the minstrels has always eluded me, but all bands proudly displayed their birthplace at the time.

Jaysus, it was a sight to behold; enough to make any man proud and many a woman hopeful for a ride in it. And, truth to tell, it played host to many hundreds of stranded ladies throughout its life (and a few lads as well).

The Demp proved as good as his word, soon opening up a new vista and range of dates for us. He secured gigs south of the border and we found we were making steady headway in towns like Dundalk, Drogheda and other big venues, but Dublin and Cork were the real targets. He knew the business and was really in tune with the spots that would be into our pop-based programme. He would never have sent us to warrior in Borris-in-Ossory.

The venues a band played were seen as an indicator of their popularity. There was a lot of competition at the time, and fulfilling the demands from all the showbands to play the big gigs led to a lot of managers having sleepless nights. We played the Orpheus in Belfast, which was the biggest statement a band could make about being a draw in Belfast. But the pressure was always on Peter to break us into Dublin.

As well as being our manager, the Demp was also our biggest fan. His passions in life were rally-driving and music. He was a man with a wicked sense of humour and held his own with the merciless banter. But if you came off stage in the Orpheus without signing the photos and talking to the punters, then you'd be looking at trouble. Like Maurice, he believed the real work began after the music stopped. You had to build a following, even if you had to do it one conversation at a time.

Every so often, he would suggest that we should be doing a bit more "Sugar Sugar" music in our programme and intimated that his job would be a lot easier if we were to do some more "black puddin'" country stuff. But Billy and the lads were not interested and much preferred the "lobster thermidor" approach. Or, at least, I thought with their sophistication they did.

I imagined that these powerful minstrels had oodles of class and talent and that somehow I, being a passenger in this great and magnificent array of musicality, would have to mind my step. I don't think I ever got over the overpowering feeling of being a lucky ducker to be standing on the same stage as them. I believe it was connected to the fact that all

I could do was sing, and these lads could all do that, equally as good as me, and play instruments as well. No one ever said anything to encourage this feeling and, in fact, there was seldom any judgment made by anyone on anyone else during this phase of the band's development. If there were any comments about a performance, it would inevitably be of a casual "well done, Bigman", or if the thing hadn't gone too well "you made a right horse's arse of that". But they had a presence that intimidated me, nonetheless.

In the old Morris death trap on wheels, it was about all a man could do to survive with any sense of sanity left intact, whatever journey lay ahead. There was no space to turn, stretch, move about or lie down. The body was always in contact with another doing exactly the same thing. The roads were in bad shape in those days and whatever about the homeward trip, where tiredness would play a part despite the odd hand of poker, the sortie out was trying, to say the least.

Journeys in the big gig-rig changed all that. Now there was not only luxury and comfort but also conversation, *craic* and any devilment a lad could get up to as well. Of a spirited nature, you might say.

Any gathering of men who are travelling, on average, a thousand miles a week, need a certain chemistry to survive. The mix in the band was helped by the fact that we came from the two differing traditions and about seven different cultures. We were, as polite people at the time remarked, a "mixed" band. Prods and Taigs, Orange and Green, Loyalist and Republican, Nationalist and Unionist, Left and Right, Lambeg and *Bodhrán* are all labels that could be applied. It was a potent brew and there was rarely a dull moment, when we got going.

Growing up in Strabane, one of my early memories is of shop windows with the notice "No Catholics need Apply". Seems ludicrous in today's world of equal opportunities, but that's the way it was. The standing joke in the town was that "even the unemployed were unemployed". They couldn't even get their usual nixers things were so bad.

At St Columb's College in Derry, I learned a bit of Irish (and a lot of English) history. There was a passionless, neutral feel to it all and if at the end of it you were a bit confused about your identity, then you wouldn't have been to blame. We used to have an English teacher who told us that the proper name for Derry was "LondonDray". That's how he pronounced it and he assured my scoffing head that this was the correct and only way.

We were fed an unflattering and unappetising menu of theological one-upmanship piffle about rival Proddie secondary schools, but the main thrust of the indoctrination was that we were right and they were wrong. It was as simple as that.

It was never openly stated that we were better than our Protestant non-fellow students, only ever that we were "right". Jesus loved us, but He had yet to make up His mind about those near-pagans. I don't think there was ever a meeting of the waters. There just never seemed to be any chance to play, sing, dance or dander with these "different" kids. There were no inter-school battles on the sporting field or, indeed, in any field. It was just not on.

This was the paradigm, with which the unenlightened leaders of our minds sought to

The original band: Back: *(left to right)* Sean Mahon, Davy McKnight, Torry Megahy, Maurice Henry. Front: *(left to right)* Billy Brown, Damien McIlroy, Derek Dean.

Playing at a Belfast funeral in the Whitla Hall, Queen's University Belfast. The lamé suits were perhaps a bit over the top.

Look out Ferrari!

There were no ballrooms open during Lent so we hit the cinemas.

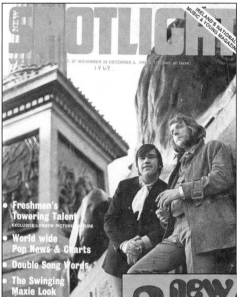

Making the cover of *Spotlight*, the top Irish entertainment magazine at the time, was one to remember. (Courtesy of Sean Mahon)

New *Spotlight* – new blood: Lindsay Looney, *(second from the left)* Ray Donnan, *(fourth from the left)* Ivan Laybourne *(fifth from the left)*… My boot just happens to be near his a**e! (Courtesy of Sean Mahon)

Top Twenty

1—Tears.—Ken Dodd.
2—Good News Week.— Hedgehoppers Anonymous.
3—Orange and Green.—Spinners
4—Yesterday Man.— Chris Andrews.
5—The Wonder of You.— Brendan Bower.
6—Evil Hearted You.— Yardbirds.
7 Here It Comes Again.— Fortunes.
8—Get Off My Cloud.— Rolling Stones.
9—If You Gotta Go.— Manfred Mann.
10—Hucklebuck Shoes.— Brendan Bowyer.
11—Eve of Destruction.— Barry McGuire.
12—Almost There.— Andy Williams.
13—La Yenka.—Derek Dean.
14—The Carnival Is Over.— Seekers.
15—Hang On Sloopy.—McCoys.
16—I Went Out With My Baby To-night.— Moses K and the Prophets.
17—Haunted House.—Joe Clarke.
18—But You're Mine.— Sonny and Cher.
19—My Own Peculiar Way.— Joe Dolan.
20—Yesterday.—Matt Monro.

October 30, 1965

1. THESE BOOTS ARE MADE FOR WALKING — Nancy Sinatra.
2. 19th NERVOUS BREAKDOWN—Rolling Stones.
3. LOVELY LEITRIM—Larry Cunningham.
4. IRELAND SWINGS—Brian Coll & Plattermen.
5. MY LOVE—Petula Clarke.
6. YOU WERE ON MY MIND—Chrispian St. Peters.
7. MAKE THE WORLD GO AWAY—Eddie Arnold.
8. SPANISH FLEA — Herb Alpert.
9. ONE KISS FOR OLD TIMES SAKE — Murty Quinn.
10. A GROOVEY KIND OF LOVE—Mind Benders.
11. MIRROR, MIRROR — Pinkerton's Assort. Colours.
12. MICHELLE—Overlanders.
13. SHA LA LA LA LE — Small Faces.
14. TOGETHER AGAIN — Dixies.
15. LOVE IS JUST A BRO. KEN HEART—Cilla Black.
16. BARBARA ANNE—Beach Boys.
17. KING COLE YENKA — Derek Dean & Freshmen.
18. IF I HAD MY LIFE TO LIVE OVER AGAIN—Eileen Reid.
19. GIRL—St. Louis Union.
20. KATHLEEN—Brian Coll & Plattermen.

1966

★ Here are Ireland's Top Ten pops of the week as played in Radio Eireann's Top Ten programme on October 25, 1965.

1	(1)	Tears	Ken Dodd	Col.
2	(3)	The Wonder of You	Brendan Bowyer	HMV
3	(2)	Eve of Destruction	Barry McGuire	RCA
4	(4)	If you gotta go, go now	Manfred Mann	HMV
5	(5)	Almost There	Andy Williams	CBS
6	(6)	Look Through Any Window	The Hollies	Parl.
7	(—)	Evil Hearted You	The Yardbirds	Col.
8	(7)	Il Silenzio	Nini Rosso	Durium
9	(8)	Message Understood	Sandy Shaw	Pye
10	(—)	La Yenka	The Freshmen	

Spotlight October 1965

The dreaded paper collar before meltdown!

Billy Brown in a suit – a rare sight indeed.

This poster was seen as daring at the time… but she was a beautiful lady.
(Courtesy of Eddie Kelly)

Promoting 'Go Granny Go'. I eventually caught her. See page 137 for details!

See page 137 for details!

Derek Dean

PERSONALITY FILE

NAME: Derek McMenamin

AGE: 22

HOMETOWN: Ballymena; flat in Belfast

DESCRIPTION: 6' 1½"; Green eyes; black hair

AGE ENTERED SHOWBIZ: 18

FORMER OCCUPATION: Student teacher

RADIO AND TV: BBC, UTV, Telefis and Radio Eireann

RECORDS: 'Gone Away,' 'I Stand Alone'

HOBBIES: Motoring, Racing, Girls

FAVOURITE ARTISTES: Peggy Lee, Brook Benton, Green-
    beats, Coasters, Beach Boys, Plattermen, Drifters,
    Regal Showbands

LIKES: Good well cooked food; ginger ale; Rolls Royces;
    meeting people

DISLIKES: Scruffy halls; income tax; religious discrimination

Derek Dean of the Freshmen is one of the few Northern singers to have a really big fan-following of his own. He is handsome, quiet and just a little shy—the formula for showband personality success. He gave up a career in the teaching profession to turn professional musician.

A clean-cut,
non-drinking man!

At one stage, we decided to dump our instruments and become maître d's…

The happy men.

the swinging
FRESHMEN
"Papa oo mow mow"

Ireland's greatest vocal team

… then we changed our minds and thought about joining the Mormons.

establish a spiritual superiority over the other side and, at the same time, prevent outright hostility and hate. It was way wide of the mark. By keeping us apart, they oiled and coiled a vital cog in the war that was destined to erupt between the two irreconcilable factions in my divided homeland: the Catholic Irish and the Protestant British.

Until the Freshmen, I had never worked, played, socialised or interacted in any way with our Protestant neighbours. I had ceased being a Catholic when I was 12, after a big bully of an uneducated priest gave me a bit of a hammering in the classroom in my first year in the Derry school. He was a warrior in a frock or, to give it its proper name, a soutane. I took a horrible slapping for something that the big gulpin thought I had done. He was wrong, but that didn't seem to matter.

Up to that day, I had bought and celebrated the whole Catholic brainwash fest. Mass on a Sunday, evening devotions, the Stations of the Cross with my mother, and all the attendant regalia involved in loving, praising and adoring a Catholic God. But when the giant basher hammered my head with his fists that day, I decided that God had dirty hands and wanted no more to do with it all. It didn't strike me at the time that this was a bit extremist, but the deed was done. I was now, in my own head, a pagan.

So after a couple of hours on the bus, it was no wonder the talk would turn to politics and the rights and wrongs of our day. We were a mixture of the bigoted, the uninterested, the read, the unread and the ignorant. There was probably a bit of all of that in each one of us, but some had, shall I say, more trenchant opinions and a greater eagerness to express them than others. It was the same on both sides of the cultural divide.

From the lads in the band who came from the Unionist tradition, there was an echo of the infamous words of Terence O'Neill. He was regarded at this time as a liberal unionist, and, like many men to follow him he really pissed off a certain Mr Paisley, who mounted his big Orange charger and initiated his "O'Neill must Go" campaign.

This leader once said when talking about Catholic people: "If a Roman Catholic is jobless and lives in a most ghastly hovel, he will rear eighteen children on national assistance. However, if you treat Roman Catholics with due consideration and kindness, they will live like Protestants in spite of the authoritative nature of their Church."

This was a fair reflection of what some of our guys were thinking as we grew and worked together. There was a delicate balance we had to strike and we did it with a good deal of banter and humour. I don't ever recall any bitterness at that stage of the band's life. But, as with most things, to quote Bobbie D, "the times they were a changin'".

I suppose we were trying to score points off each other, but we were bonded by something that was much more powerful than religious bigotry or political bias. We were all driven men: driven by the music.

So what was the music and where did it come from?

The five-hour gigs made it impossible to be anything other than a cover band. I don't imagine there's an outfit anywhere on the planet that could perform for this length of time and do an all-original set. So it was ordained, not just for the Freshmen but for all the travelling troubadours throughout the land. Learn and rehash the current hits and, interestingly, do them as near to the original record as possible. The challenge lay in achieving an identical replication. It was as if we were trying to tell the audiences, "Listen to this folks, we can do this song every bit as good as the Beatles, Elvis, Chuck Berry, Buddy Holly, Acker Bilk and the rest. You're never going to get to see these guys anyway, so lap it up off the bandstand here; you're missing nothing."

And the paying customers loved every minute of it. They didn't particularly wish to listen to original music. The biggest reception went to the biggest hits of the day, as long as they were rendered just as they had been recorded. The appreciation of the music was based on this ability to replicate the original. If it wasn't delivered to the punter's ear in exactly the same sound pattern as the record, then you were no good. And this, more than anything else, was the reason for a lack of originality in the music back then: there was no demand for it. And why bother, when this stuff was paying the rent and all the rest. If a man tried to autograph a song with his own special contribution to its beauty, he'd receive a bit of a deafener.

One example of this sticks in my mind.

In 1962, Acker Bilk had a major hit with the wistful melody "Stranger on the Shore". He wrote it originally for his daughter and it became the theme music for a children's TV show shortly afterwards. As a result of this lucky break, the tune became a worldwide smash. It was performed on the B flat clarinet and a good few of the bands played it. The thing was made for Brown.

He gave it a breathy rendition and stuck to the original melody line and it was favourably received. He then decided, one night, that he would add a vocal to the instrumental, and that too went well.

Then he upped the ante. He would play it on the liquorice stick with a little improvisation, a little jazz feel, and he would sing it and take some liberty with the melody line. Now this was a real delight. He brought a lover's feel to the piece and his voice went up the waves and down the shoreline, very gently and respectfully. He added a touch of Brown magic to the work and it was a thrill to hear him do it so effortlessly. The backing chords, of course, remained the same, but his vocal variations were those of a master.

But, in general, the dancers didn't like it. There was a suspicious response from the floor to this strange version of the Bilk hit. "What are you at? What are you doing to this wonderful tune; can you not sing and play it properly?" was the reaction. And very little applause would result. The obvious lesson was that, North and South, there wasn't a big market for an original approach. But this attitude only drove Billy on.

Each night "Stranger on the Shore" would become stranger to their ears. The melodic variations would become more pronounced and the timing of his phrases would linger and rest, until you imagined that he must break time. But he would only be teasing. He never, ever, made a mistake. And each night he would play a different solo and sing a different tune, with not one discordant note against the backing chords. He played and sang it

like a brand-new song at every gig. You had a sort
of feeling: "Good man, Bill; keep her lit."

It didn't please the Demp, of course, but that
didn't worry the man from Larne. He was out of
the northeastern port, but his spirit wafted across
the oceans from New York's East Side, or maybe
Basin Street, New Orleans. Somewhere in the ether,
it encountered a Celtic up-swell from the Scottish
Highlands and lingered with it awhile, before settling
on this unheralded Northern backwater as a birthing
place. There was a bit of California too, but that
wouldn't surface for a while yet.

In this, as in every version of the Freshmen he
played in, Bill was the main man. But there were
some dangerous lads alongside him too.

Sean Mahon played trombone like a man making
love to his adoring wife, and he blew the trumpet
like a teenage lover with a hard-on that would not go
down. And that's a difficult thing to do physically. I
mean the musical challenge, of course, and it would
be fair to say that this mighty man faced many of
them.

The embouchure (the way a brass man shapes his
lips) is totally different for both these instruments.
He has to blow and spit into a tiny round bell. There
is nothing to help him; it's all done by tongue and
blow. It's fairly commonplace to see a musician who
doubles on tenor and baritone or alto sax and clarinet.
The wind instruments have a reed they use to help
soften their cough.

But trombone and trumpet being blown by the
same mouth is highly unusual. Sean didn't play them
at the same time, naturally, but he wasn't a man
for half measures. His eyes stood out to a dizzying

level when he blew the horn, and a man would think they were about to pop. After a lung-draining, ball-breaking set of phrases, he would return to his rhythmic dance, something you frequently see in people who are lost in the music.

He had started singing in the band and, as we all suspected, was a real showman. He certainly could handle a song, and to say he put his heart and soul into every rendition would be near enough the truth. With a pitch awareness that was unerring, he proved a dab hand when it came to singing harmony as well.

Some people have a presence onstage, and some have to force it. Mahon was a natural and he moved to this seductive rhythm like an experienced lover who would never miss a trick or a beat. His dancing in the brass line gave a lot of joy to the thousands of onlookers who would pay their money to see him. Sean blew and blew and danced and danced, and they loved it.

In those days, in the early 1960s, Sean wore funny hats for a musician. They were like the Tony Hancock little-Englander version, with a feather stuck in the brim, and they portrayed a somewhat conservative image, completely at odds with the reality of this particular Freshman. He lived in Downpatrick and had previously played with the Johnny Mitchell Showband. His hunger to succeed was one of the main driving forces in the band and he wouldn't settle for less than perfection. When you watched the Freshmen, it was impossible to ignore Sean. He was the consummate professional.

Davy McKnight thundered on the drums. Jaysus, he was a skinny guy – he still is – but when he hit the skins, the place rattled. All drummers are eccentric and Davy was no exception. He was blessed with a zany sense of humour and I think I laughed more with him than with all the others combined. At rehearsals, the Belfast boogaloo rocker would play very handy. Mostly he would just play on the snare when we were learning a new tune, but when it came to live action you could be sure the joint would jump and pagan demons would be abroad looking for new converts. There are drummers who make a man go wild and there are some who make a man go to sleep, and Davy would keep you awake all night. He was a marvellously talented singer as well.

Davy's voice was comfortable singing anywhere between tenor and falsetto. He was another lad who could belt it out and did so on three or four songs at each gig. He sang harmony too and, as the man says, he never missed a beat: fairly important if you're the drummer. After Billy and Sean, I would reckon that he had the next biggest base of dedicated fans, all just interested in him. There's something extra special in watching a drummer who is rocking and singing at the same time. Common enough to see guitars and pianists do it, but the drums are a different matter. I think there's a bit of the feeling that although it's great to listen to the magic sounds he's making, there's the added relief that the bastard doesn't live upstairs or next door. Maybe that's what it is.

You certainly wouldn't have wanted Davy living upstairs, or on the same street, come to that.

He laid down a law that for the band to rock, it was vital for the bass guitar and the kick drum to play together. And, lucky for us, we had a man who did just that.

Torrance (Torry) Megahy was the four-string bass man and, here again, particularly amongst musicians in other bands, he had a following all of his own. I used to think that he spent most of his money on new guitar gear. He lived in Ballymena, but didn't have the Scottish twang and lilt. To say that he spent a lot of dough on equipment is some testament to his love of the instrument and his dedication to being the best in the business, especially when you understand that men from Ballymena, and probably women too, have the reputation of being ultra tight.

And Torry could sing it out with the best of them. He wrote some and had a fairly good ear for what latest release was coming good and what songs wouldn't make it.

But we always seemed to be at loggerheads with one another. I never seemed to be able to relax around him. He was fond of sticking his face right into yours when he spoke, and his eyes would be up there in your eyeballs with an unnerving intensity. He never did anything to me and it's very difficult to describe how it was, but it was awkward to say the least.

I believe there is a vibration that is a constant in all relationships. It changes over time, and the relationship changes with it. When it doesn't change, it dies. I somehow feel that the vibration between this man and me couldn't echo, right from the start. There was no resonance, just a stagnant, still, slimy pond of mutual indifference with no chance of a ripple of revival. The only constant in life is change and it would be true to say that the brilliant bass man would always be on a different track than myself. And when our paths crossed, it could be painful.

But his playing added massively to the sound of the band; there is no denying that. And when he fingered throbbing bass rhythms and patterns on the low note bedrock of the wall of sound, there was no discomfort. It went as it was meant to go: solid, aggressive, "keep your feet off the floor 'cos I'm lighting a fire with these bastard notes" kind of stuff.

There is potential in every great pop song for a bass moment. Not the patterned riff or line, which is underneath the melody, vital though that is. It is revealed by great players at the precise moment; the subconscious ear demands it. It's like a pat on the head for a task well done. You're not expecting it, but when it comes it's, let's say, very pleasant. Megahy would do it again and again. He was a natural. Other bass men would come on their night off to hear him, and that was about as big a compliment as was going at the time. All bass players – in fact, all musicians – know that the secret of success is playing the right notes in the right place at the right time. The Ballymena bass man was a master.

In any body of men there is a differing stratum of friendships and interactions. Some get on well together; others co-exist and work in the name of a common cause but rarely bother to socialise or make friends with each other. The band was exactly the same.

When you're all the time living in each other's inside pocket, it's a miracle that, whatever it is, gets done at all. Mile after mile after mile after mile of living together in a confined space up and down the country becomes a real friendship-buster, but in general, sanity prevailed.

Sometimes though, we had to invent our own amusement in the wee small hours, in the never-ending treks up and down, North and South, east and west and backwards, until you met yourself coming forwards across the land. As we broke new ground, the journeys naturally became longer and the monotony of it was enough to drive a man round the bend – literally round thousands of them. We would rarely talk about music, and playing it was, normally, out of the question.

So we invented "The Theatre of the Talking Arse". The four main characters in this extravaganza were played by Davy, Billy and myself. I played twins.

We would write out our scripts and rehearse them at the beginning of the journey and then, before terminal boredom would strike during the journey, say about three hours in, we would shout "Halt the Wagon for the Arse Theatre". Brakes rammed on and lights fully up, two bare behinds would be stuck over the second last seat towards the rear of the wagon and the playlet would begin. Sometimes one of the talking holes would be smoking and this proved to be quite a tricky task. It was inevitably a man talking to his wife over a garden fence and it never failed to arouse hysteria amongst the demented minstrels. The third actor, not actually participating in that night's show, would act as prop hand and be responsible for the lit cigarettes and other decorations, such as headscarves wrapped around the wife's bare behind.

A performance could last for five minutes and the scripts were nearly always adhered to, as ad-libbing was guaranteed to produce chaos. There was the smart arse, and the silly hole. They were the standard characters and you'd be amazed at the amount of variations we managed on those two themes. Maybe not. If you imagine a trans-Atlantic flight twice a day, six days a week, you come near to understanding the agony in the wagon. Not forgetting, of course, the show in between. Nobody came to see the Freshmen to hear about the dismal trip down to whatever neck of the woods we would be playing, and everybody had their own worries after the music stopped. So we delved into a wee bit of insanity to preserve whatever sanity we had.

There was another hilarious entertainment, which has been fairly common among young men for some time: fart-lighting.

The trick was to drop the strides, hunker over and hold a lighter up to the anal opening and, as the belly gas hit the air, light the Zippo. Not all of the men experimented with this, but there was one super champion. His lit emissions whooshed a trail of blue and silver smoke right down the bus. The rest of the contenders foostered and farted in vain attempts to match his magnificence, but all comers failed. Who was that man? Who else but Billy.

But there was one Freshman for whom this constant journeying was a serious ordeal. Imagine suffering from travel sickness and working in a touring band. That was the fate of our guitar player, Damien McIlroy, or as he was known, the Dane.

I used to watch him smash his guitar against his amplifier and speaker in the middle of a frantic solo and wonder if this flight from sanity was somehow connected to the poor man's plight in the wagon. Bowling along at breakneck speed, we would suddenly hear the shout of "Stop, pull her in!", and the Dane would be out the front door, throwing up at the side of the road. He was what you could describe as a "highly strung" youth, and during any journey you could tell that the next bolting episode wasn't too far away by observing him toss and turn in his seat at the front of the rig.

The malaise, however, didn't prevent him playing his guitar into your head. He was the best rhythm-guitar player I had heard and was no slouch when it came to playing lead either. When he caught fire with a solo, there would be no stopping him. There was a flight of fancy up into the stratosphere and the thing with strings slung around his neck and sticking out in front of his crotch, became a second cock. He waved it legally at the excited onlookers and made it squeal. He got a good few of them excited too. From Randalstown in County Antrim, but also living in Larne, Damien was probably the hardest worker in the band. He was also the proud owner of one of the strongest falsetto voices in the land, a really powerful vocal screamer, something that we would use in the years to come.

Maurice Henry was the bandleader. He was older and wiser than the rest of us and was the only married man at that time. His first love was the euphonium, the beautiful, mellow horn that he would play with a tone that could have serenaded a pregnant nun. Maurice blew with soft lips. His lungs breathed a pure air down into the pipe of the classical instrument, and this resulted in beautifully rounded notes wafting out from the bell. He won many prizes down the years for his mastery of the smooth delivery, and his tonguing skills were much admired.

Being a true son of Ballymena, he was as tight as a fish's arse. This fact worked greatly to our communal advantage as, when he would go for payment after the gig, he would haggle over the last penny. When it came to paying hotel bills and the like, you could be sure that there was no mistake on the bill. Our bandleader wouldn't have tolerated it. No way. It was against his religion.

And, as I have already highlighted, there was a lot that he wouldn't ignore. Punctuality was one of his main demands. You had to be on time or there was hell to pay. Not just on time for the wagon's departure, but for the stage call, the rehearsal, photo sessions and so on. It didn't matter who was involved; his justice was fair and balanced. And it seemed that he saw everything; a man could get away with nothing. It was he whom the Demp reported to with dates, fees and all the rest of the business that just kept growing and growing along with the band.

And he handled his Selmer Mk.6 tenor sax with a respectful fluency. I imagine blowing at the side of Master Brown was mainly inspiration, tinged with a touch of intimidation. The stem of our bandleader's saxophone was as the day it had left the factory in Oregon, but standing beside him, blowing down the same mike, was Brown's identical instrument, featuring an assortment of multi-coloured elastic bands, delicately positioned to hold the saxophone's pads in place. Our leader was also known to lift the trumpet, but not in the same manic style of the young blood Mahon. They only ever did a two-trumpet piece on very rare occasions, and I think there was a mini war between the two of them as to who should play what. It was never going to be a recipe for harmony.

I said Maurice was a bit wiser than the rest of us. He was a family man, and in the years since I don't think I ever came across a musician as dedicated to his wife and family. He might have been tight with the folding stuff, but he was generous in every other way. On many nights he put us up in his home when, for one reason or another, we couldn't make it back to where we normally put the head down. He was a mine of knowledge about the game, which he was more than willing to share, and he was the first man I ever heard use the verb "to tramp". "Did ye tramp her, Bigman?" was the first thing he'd ask upon your arrival back to the bus before the run home. "What do you think, Maurice?" was the inevitable reply, regardless of how you fared.

That was the Freshmen. Throw in a promotional company with the ominous sounding name of Pentagon Promotions, run by the late Vincent Hannah, whose gofer was a young, starry-eyed Belfast groupie and eager learner by the name of Sammy Smyth, and you have a fair idea of what it was all about. We had recorded a couple of original songs in London, which were released on some label or other with gusto and anticipation. But the gusto soon disappeared and the anticipation was put on a slower burn.

Back in those days there was no real prospect of making any money out of record sales. The sole purpose was to have it played on the radio. And there was no expectation either of making a fortune from performing and composer royalty payments.

"I Stand Alone" was a dirge that I wrote with a pal at the Ranch and it was my first serious attempt at songwriting. All very sincere and intense, it was a magnificent flop.

We needed a hit record. And it was on its way.

NINE

La Yenka

The Demp was adamant that it was going to take a hit record to work the magic and establish us as a big band in the South. By now we were setting fires in an ever-widening circle and it was agreed that a hit record would put the top hat on it. But what would we record? Would we try and establish some kind of sound of our own, and what would that be? We had gotten over the first few humps, as it were, but were now genuinely seeking an identity.

It's OK to be a travelling jukebox with the ability to turn your hand to nearly anything, but when it comes to making a statement we didn't know what to do. Or, at least, there was no one musical imperative that was shouting back at us: "Me. Me. Follow Me. I am what you are". We were everything. We might have tried to play better than everyone else, but they were doing exactly the same thing. There were only so many times you could use the word "fabulous" before people got sick of it.

Billy, as musical director, had many talents but this wasn't one of them. We all wrote songs, of course, and our MD unsurprisingly wrote the best 'uns, but they never seemed to be worth sticking your neck out for and declaring, "Hold on lads, I want you all to listen to this, as I really believe that this is the kind of stuff we should be concentrating on." To this day I can't work out why this pertained. There was enough songwriting talent amongst those lads to write hit after hit, and it was just completely ignored. I have a feeling that talk of "black puddin', fillin' the halls, doin' the punter stuff", all that manager speak, had a malign effect on the creative juices of the early Freshmen, but even that is a weak enough explanation.

The band decided to change my name and wanted to call it Derek and the Freshmen. We were travelling home from a gig in the South and the matter was raised. This is exactly how it went.

Maurice, who was driving began, "Bigman, the Demp says, and I agree with him, that we should call the band Derek something and the Freshmen, but not McMenamin. Nobody can pronounce it. What do you think?"

"I know," shouted Mahon. "Call him Cave Mann, you know, like Manfred Mann. He's a big fuckin' caveman for sure and that would sound good, Cave Mann and the Freshmen."

I didn't engage as I thought the thing was just a piss-take to while away another hour of the trip.

"Naw," replied Megahy. "We should call him Cave Hill, after the mountain. That's better."

And so the debate continued as to whether I should be called a caveman or a mountain man. They were laughing their balls off.

"Fuck off, the lot of you," was my reply. "Derek McMenamin is a great name."

"We could call him Yehudi McMenamin," laughed one of the others.

"James Dean," was Brown's contribution. "Call him Derek Dean."

A couple of nights later a new set of handouts were delivered to plug the band and that was the first time I saw the name Derek Dean. Derek Dean and the Freshmen. Simple as that.

I bought my first car, a Corsair GT; I couldn't yet drive but would take it to gigs near Belfast and it afforded a bit of sexual freedom. It was a decent enough motor but the week after I bought it Ford brought out a newer version, which our publicist Vincent Hannah bought. "It's far faster, Bigman," said he. "It's a V4."

We had a gig in Cork the following weekend and it was agreed that we would swap the two cars and if I thought his was indeed better, then I would trade my own in and get the newer version.

But I wrote it off and decapitated a horse in, above all places, the village of Horse and Jockey. There were four of us in the car. I was driving, the Demp was in the front passenger seat and Billy and Torry sat in the back. We were flying down the road in the early morning, having left Bangor in County Down after the Saturday night gig there and were driving overnight, straight to Cork.

I woke up in Our Lady of Lourdes Hospital in Cashel and was greeted with an angelic, smiling face. She looked like an angel – that is if angels wear the stiffened collars and hoods this lady was sporting – and as she leaned carefully over the bed, she whispered in gentle tones: "Would you like a bottle?"

"Aw, no thanks, I don't drink," was my amazed reply, whereupon she tittered merrily in her black and sexless uniform.

"I mean, do you want to use the toilet; do you want to pee?" she giggled, and I closed my eyes and went back to sleep.

The Dixielanders with Joe Mac and the lads had come across the dead horse and the unconscious minstrel and drove me to the hospital. I was the only one hurt in those pre-seatbelt days and the boys continued on to Cork and did the gig without me. It was fine.

I left the hospital the next day and headed back up North, but about two weeks later when I was getting out of a chair there was a mighty snap in my neck. It happened in Horse and Jockey, but it was just now presenting pain. It was a right pain in the neck made even bigger when I had to pay for the car. There was some hassle about the insurance and it took cash money to sort it. The body healed back to full strength after about six weeks, the collar was discarded, and the next big thing was a holiday in Italy with Davy.

Our drummer had become my best mate in the band. I stayed at his home for a while and we worked, lived and played together.

On the wall of his parent's home in Windsor Drive there was a portrait of Elizabeth Windsor in all her glory. His Da had been a Special Forces soldier, the

B Specials, I mean, and he was much bemused and amused at the whole idea of his darlin' son making his crust in a band. He had a healthy disrespect for its future prospects and that, in truth, was what my own parents believed. Music is alright to listen to, but it's no profession, especially as both their lads had turned down teaching jobs. Davy's family was amazed to meet a Taig who ate meat on a Friday.

His mother smothered Davy with love and she gave me a mighty welcome too. She was a magnificent cook and fed us like the warriors we felt we were. But living in a terraced house in the shadow of Windsor Park was a long way from Strabane. It was every bit as friendly, though, and I was never made feel anything other than at home. Some things are all in the head, and feeling comfortable in a B Special's home in Belfast with the Queen smiling down on you was, shall I say, a challenge. The old indoctrination was clinging on for its cheap life, but it couldn't survive for long in the presence of such hospitality.

Not that Davy and I hung about anywhere for too long. We shared a lot of things, the most memorable of which was a dark-featured, ghost-like, gothic princess we called "Pour it into me". This was her love cry, which would begin in a barely audible whisper and, with mounting penetration, would gradually grow in volume until any passers-by would imagine she was being tried for treason and the execution by poison was being hysterically defied. "Pour it into me," was her demanding scream as she became more animated, coming to the end of the passion. She would shout it out in a shrill voice that broke into a sigh and then an embarrassed silence.

"Pour it into me" knew what and whom she liked and was expert at providing for her pressing needs.

I thought Davy was uncomfortable when hearing about the great fun I'd had with this dark-haired lover the previous night in her flat in the north of the city. There couldn't possibly be two "pour" addicts in the same town, and I couldn't believe it when he interrupted my tale and described exactly what went down. As it turned out, we wouldn't be the only two in the organisation to be presented with the liquid request. She was living proof of the old saying "Good girls go to Heaven, but bad girls go everywhere". Her kindest favour was to make you believe that it was you, and you alone, who fulfilled the deepest need. This was her compassion for a horny fool; her blessing. And it was clear that this lady, with her beautiful long black hair and never-ending slender legs, could go anywhere on earth she decided for a refill.

The holiday in Italy was to mark the end of my non-drinking days. Here I was, at twenty-one, full of *craic*, full of the music, full of cum and full of about every good thing a man could want. But I didn't take a drink. There was no need; I wasn't shy and I didn't have any hang-ups about getting up on stage and letting rip in front of anyone. The bigger the crowd the better, was my way of thinking. I never could see where the enjoyment was in sitting down in pubs and drinking pint after pint. It just didn't appeal. I had seen thousands of drunk men who were seriously disadvantaged in all sorts of ways, and I never had the slightest inclination to join their ranks. But Italy would change all that.

"You're not going to let me drink for the next two weeks all on my own, Bigman," were the words which greeted me as we sat down at a roadside café in the little seaside town of Cattolica.

"That pledge you took is out of date now and, anyway, you can go back off it when we return to the city."

So here I was with my best mate, on holiday in a foreign land, and still there was a distinct reticence about taking a glass of wine. It was stronger than that; it was a sense of foreboding. It was the wisdom of the ages shouting down at me to desist, to stay away from the stuff; let Davy drink on his own, don't be a fool. I'm sure most people don't have this sensation before their first tipple, but it happened with me.

"For fuck's sake, be a man and take a drink with me."

"Go on, then, but I'll be back off it when we go home, like you said."

And I drank my first glass of ethyl alcohol. Davy poured and I raised a toast to a great time, to loads of women and *craic* and to our stated intention of improving Italian-Irish relations in the bedding stakes. It was a sweet, sickly, shitty wine called Asti Spumante and it was the greatest disappointment I think I ever had.

"Jaysus, Davy, where's the buzz?"

"Here, have another; it's not bad."

We finished the bottle and ordered another and another after that. But nothing happened. It was a major letdown and I couldn't see or feel anything different than drinking three or four sweet drinks on the trot.

We got a fourth bottle and the drummer man assured me that the high was coming.

"Drink this one and I doubt if we'll need another," was his prediction, but we did. I remember ordering a seventh bottle and sitting down at the table after visiting the toilet. As I pulled the chair into the table, I noticed that the guy who had been sitting at the table opposite me for the past hour or so with his wife had the biggest and funniest nose I'd ever seen on a human being. It hadn't occurred to me before, but now I couldn't stop giggling. And worse, I stood up and pointed at it.

I took another swig from the bottle and roared with laughter. Jaysus, what a schnozz. Jimmy Durante had nothing on this man and I wanted the whole town of Cattolica to come and marvel at it.

Another slug out of the neck of the bottle and my head began to swim backwards against itself and I started to swagger.

The poor man and his wife must have been really pissed off with this big animal of an Irish drunk howling with glee at his poor *nez*.

But then the lights went out. I had just experienced my first and last buzz from the drink. I would spend a long time chasing it, dedicate a lot of man hours to its search and spend a whole load of the green stuff in the futile quest. But I wasn't to know that then and it all appeared to be great fun.

"Ah, Bigman, you're some *craic* sober, but drunk you're magic."

I'll never forget those words uttered the next morning by the Freshmen's stickman.

"I never thought you'd stop with the women. I never saw you dance like that before. It was magic.

We'll have some more of that tonight."

I genuinely didn't know what he was talking about. I could remember nothing and any bits I could involved drinking wine at a café and seeing a man with a funny nose. But it was all fragmented. I didn't recall our meal, the trip back to the hotel, the trip out to the nightclub or any of the other stuff that Davy found so enjoyable. My mouth was very dry and I was dying for a drink of water, but apart from a foul-tasting tongue I wasn't in bad shape.

"I'll tell you one thing, head, you might have just started, but you can sure handle your liquor."

"Oh yeah, well it's not that strong. Maybe we can try something a bit stronger tonight."

We went to one of the biggest clubs in the area and were sitting around, drinking more Italian wine and eyeing up whatever talent was on show. I was taking it a bit handier with the wine, but was drinking as much as Davy. It was still over-sweet and not particularly palatable, but I was determined that my next one would be something different. Anything but this piss.

We were chatting about facing a couple of likely targets when the band struck up and the entire club stood as one, emitted shrieks of delight to the sound coming from the stage and rushed onto the club's dance floor. It was a stampede. We were the only two not on the floor and they proceeded to perform this weird dance, all the while whooping and hollering. We were listening to the opening bars of our first hit record.

La Yenka. La what? La Yenka.

When the band finished, they roared for more. We looked on in amazement and we both realised at that moment that we had our hit. This was what we had been looking for. If it was having this effect on the Italian crowd, then surely it would do the same in Ireland. Sure hadn't "The Hucklebuck" recently been a massive success for Brendan Bowyer and the Royal?

After the show, I approached the band and bought a copy of the disc. My head was buzzing with the thought of recording it for home and Davy agreed that we were onto something big.

In the following week I went through the card with my selection of beverages. I couldn't find one I fancied and, more importantly, couldn't find one that fancied me, but I wasn't too worried. Every time I took a drink, I wouldn't be able to remember it the next day anyway. So where was the problem? Some tasted better than others, and gin was the only one that made me sick.

The other remaining highlight of that memorable visit to the Adriatic coast was an erotic adventure at sea. I met a German lady in one of the clubs and left her home to her hotel. It was a promising encounter and she seemed as keen as me to sample our mutual pleasure zones. But her father or someone was staying in the room beside hers and she wouldn't risk rousing him. She was certainly arousing me and we agreed to meet at the beach the following afternoon. For some reason she would not entertain the idea of visiting my place, but agreed to go for a ride in one of the paddleboats that were for hire all along the beachfront.

She was wearing the tightest beach shorts I had ever lusted to get into. Her blonde hair and German green eyes added to her beauty and she smiled a winning, willing smile.

Right, thought I, we'll head out and get a bit from the shore and maybe we can celebrate our connection on the open sea. The serpent was peeping out of the top of my shorts at my beautiful companion and was encouraging me to pedal like mad and ensure we got far enough out so as not to be disturbed.

Grope, pedal, kiss, grope some more, fondle, rest, rub, tongue, lick, pedal, giggle and soon we were out of sight.

The beast was throbbing and the sea was bobbing and the serpent let out a mighty roar of approval as he was invited into a new and hungry continental sin centre. We both got a bit excited and things were getting into hand when the paddleboat lurched on the crest of a sudden wave and landed us both in the sea. We were locked in passion and it was something of a shock and a bit of a passion-killer to be taking in huge mouthfuls of salt water. The embrace was broken.

My lissome lady friend made it back to our little liner with no difficulty, but I had never learned to swim and the harder I tried to get back the further my flailing arms took me away. The serpent had abandoned ship completely and was nowhere to be seen or felt. The two dominating thoughts in my mind at that precise moment were that I wanted to get back into where I'd been and that I wanted not to drown. I think the beast provided the biggest motivator. My mouth was filling once again with water when the lovely *fräulein* turned the craft around and helped me in.

We laughed, but the surrender moment was gone. The paddling gondola was now pointed

back to shore and that's where we were headed
when the cobra raised his beautiful head again.
"But what about me?" was his urgent and by-now
greedy demand. The hungry thing had been teased,
promised, caressed and was about to let out his war
cry when the wave hit. He pounded on my shorts,
but she was having no more of the full-blown sexual
extravaganza (though she did give him an oral
examination on the homeward journey). It was the
most satisfying test he'd been through since that
unforgettable ground-breaking evening in Killybegs
at the side of the hearse. Doubtless the near-drowning
experience added to his enjoyment.

When Davy and I got back to Belfast, we
persuaded the rest of the lads that the song we'd
discovered in Italy was going to put us firmly on
the road to the big time. This was our breakthrough
record; this would make us a fortune.

They hated the thing, of course; it was just a
piece of continental pastry with very little filling and
absolutely no taste. Not to their liking, anyway. They
were spot on, but they hadn't seen the reaction of the
clubbers in Italia. We had this advantage and so we
pressed home our point with determination. They
relented. I had written a lyric that explained how to
do this simpleton dance and that rhymed. That was
all that was required.

> Everybody come and do the Yenka,
> Everybody, one, two, three.
> Everybody come and do the Yenka
> You can do it just like me.
> Left foot, left foot,
> Right foot, right foot,

> Forward, backwards,
> One, two, three,
> Nothing to it, anyone can do it,
> Come and do the Yenka, just like me.

It's not exactly what you would call a challenging lyric. There's not a pile of depth to it. The phrase "nothing to it" just about sums it up.

We recorded it in Dublin at the Eamon Andrews Studios in Henry Street and we did as good a job on it as the song would allow. We put in harmony, melodica, trombone and a couple of saxes. We also added in some mad party whoops and ye haws and yaboyas, just to give it an extra bit of spice. The late Michael Hand, who was a columnist with *Spotlight* magazine at the time, did a lot of the "atmosphere sound effects". This was a serious venture and we planned a major campaign with demonstrations of the dance steps printed out on special handouts that we gave out at all the dances.

It was generally regarded, musically, as the worst thing the band ever did, but it provided us with our hit. We became the first Northern band ever to have a song enter the Southern charts. That sounds good, but the reality was that the charts had only been in existence for a couple of years. And someone or other was fiddling them every week.

Some big names from England and from points further afield came over to dance it and join in the Yenka fun. Cathy McGowan, who was a hot number on the BBC, visited us along with the mind-blowing principal dancer with the Harlequin Ballet, by the name of Belinda Wright, and they demonstrated the intricacies of this neo-Cossack, foot-kicking polka.

It became a kind of "in-thing" to have your photo taken dancing the Yenka. It became cool to be silly. None of us could ever understand why, but we kept the ball rolling for as long as we could. There were photos of nuns dancing the Yenka in school, holding onto the children's hands, and others of record company executives dancing it in their offices. The thing went down a bomb.

As well as being a big hit in Ireland – North and South – it was a minor success in the UK charts. It got as high as 55 in the Top 100, but it certainly wasn't something I would have expected to enhance the musical reputation of this wonderful bunch of minstrels. I mean, it wasn't something you would go around boasting about, and it didn't help us with the identity problem.

We had copied another act again, but this time it wasn't an American soul singer or a big balladeer, it was continental cornball and another Irish showband. We were cashing in on the craze exploited, first of all, by the Royal with "The Hucklebuck". The new dance craze was a winning formula, so let's get one and get it out there. And we were lucky that we managed to claim the Yenka phenomenon for ourselves. A couple of other bands had heard the thing as well and had the same idea as ourselves. The Victors Showband with Art Supple had a version of it, and at least one other band of trendsetters was pipped at the post.

When the compilations of old showband hits are made nowadays, nearly forty years later, it brings back lots of happy memories, but a man could never stand up and proclaim it as his contribution to the music scene. It wasn't ours, anyway; we were only to blame for the words. I have no idea who wrote the music, what there is of it.

Billy would rant and rave about this "load of mad-dog shite" when it was called during the night. It was hard to convince the Larne man that we owed it and that it merited our best effort. It was he who played the melodica on the record, of course, and he arranged it as well, but Mr Brown would have none of it. It would be fair to say, however, that he didn't refuse the extra money we were raking in.

What about the money?

From the very first night I ever sang with the band, I thought the money was great. As a young fella getting paid to do what I would have gladly done for nothing, I had never lost the belief that this was a very fair arrangement. And I had no responsibilities. The only one I could think of was to spend it.

We heard about the massive amounts being made by our major rivals, like the Royal, the Miami, the Dixies, the Platters, the Cadets, the Capitol, the Clippers (although their heyday was over), Johnny Flynn, The Pussyeaters and The Pimps.

You might not have heard of the last two, but this was just their pseudonym and in fact they packed a lot of the ballrooms. I'd hate you to get the impression that it was all clean-cut in those days.

So, as far as I was concerned, it was a matter of pride to get onto the same rung of the financial ladder as these greats, and not purely a lust for the green stuff. I was hooked on the altogether more powerful drug, the most addictive demon breeder of all, fame. My motivation was to make the Freshmen the number fucking one band in the land. I don't use the expletive loosely here. It was clear in my consciousness that to become the number fucking one band, you had to become the top band. It was simple. I really wanted to be a famous fucker, in every way. Sure that was where the real *craic* lay.

And in the months and years after the Yenka broke our duck in the charts, the difference in the lolly became very apparent. The Demp was as good as his word; we had the black puddin' hit, and he delivered the dough. It was a sellout that we all bought into, even though there were differing reasons for the sale.

And it's lovely having your pockets stuffed with big rolled up bundles of notes. They would be tied together with elastic bands and would come in lots of five bundles of twenty each. I used to get the money off Maurice and stick it into the inside pocket of whatever jacket I'd be wearing. There was no counting for me; I took whatever the bossman gave and was thrilled skinny. We had money to burn.

I was living in a flat in Belfast by now and was slightly undomesticated. Instead of washing clothes, I would buy new ones. I'd just peel some notes from the inside pocket and buy whatever I needed, or indeed, wanted. With the fear of counting the proceeds, I became an expert at feeling it. I could tell how long it would last merely by its touch, by its bulk and shape. There was never any worry about running out of the stuff, as you knew that by the next night Maurice would be handing you another wodge to keep you going. It was now five and sometimes six nights a week, so the money train never stopped rolling.

The infrastructure that had been absent at the beginning of the 1960s was now firmly in place and new venues, recording studios and the like were opening up all over. There were new photographers and magazines and they were doing great business. It would have been impossible to have made it so big with the Yenka were it not for all this new talent, and it would continue to grow and eventually outpace the bands that had set the standards in the first place.

We used just two photographers: one in the North and one in Dublin. There was always a great demand for band photos after gigs, and in the mad scramble to get a snap and have it signed, there was always the chance of opening a decent preamble with Madame Joy.

Some of the lads, desperately chasing the free handouts, got greedy and would demand two or three or four or five or ten and it was inevitable that some nights when you'd be taking a leek after the gig you'd be piddlin' on your own photo.

You never urinated on yourself, of course, but there was always the chance of a laugh when you dribbled down on the face of someone who had, let's say, pissed you off that night.

We were well into the mid-1960s. There was no real sense of direction, just the vague notion that we were definitely headed for the top. There was a hit record and lots of money, but we were still a fair way from the number one. When we played in Cork, Rory Gallagher and his band would support us and we wondered how such an outrageous guitar maestro could be working on the undercard. He gravitated towards Billy and the pair struck up a mutual admiration society.

In Banbridge one night Van Morrison played support, with him screaming a spine-tingling set of original songs down the mike, wearing a boiler suit. It was apparent to us all that this guy was something else, but the fact that he was playing support wasn't overlooked. We were further up the ladder than this future superstar, and it didn't appear that his way was working. But we knew that something was missing from our own act as well.

This band needed something extra. We had gone as far as it seemed possible to go, with me out front and a traditional showband line-up of singer and backing band. I was, I suppose, doing my best to be as good as Brendan Bowyer, and the lads could point to the fact that we had a lot of other good things going for us as well. But that extra ingredient – the sound, the style, whatever it was – we didn't have it. Unknown to ourselves we were following a fashion, knitting a pattern.

Up to then, the formula in Ireland had been that you got a fairly dynamic, sexy, talented, crowd-pleasing, inoffensive, harmless, trustworthy, clean-cut, singing sensation and put a band of not-so noteworthy musicians behind him. It was acceptable for them to have their own fan base but they were not to seriously annoy or detract from the holy man up front.

The Freshmen had broken that paradigm in a couple of ways, notably through the presence of Brother Brown, but also in the genuine talent of a couple of the others.

I felt I fell a long way short of the requirements listed above and would always work ultra hard to compensate for it. What was missing in gifts from the Creator was made up for with watts galore of energy. I remember being asked in an interview by a pseudosophisticated London pop columnist from the *New Musical Express* what was my role in the band.

"I'm the highest paid ball-waver in Ireland," was my reply.

"The what?" he retorted.

"I'm paid to wave my balls at the ladies, to make them scream."

He laughed with me, but there was a degree of truth in it.

The band had it all, but no one individual had it all.

I had the chutzpah and the waving gonads; Brown had all the gifts that even the most greedy of men could desire; Mahon had the cabaret presence of a well-oiled lounge lizard; McIlroy had the nervous tension emitted to everybody on and off stage; McKnight had the ability to put thunder in your head as you tried to go wild; Megahy had the belly thumpin' sound vibrations that would run down the leg of your trousers and Henry had a calm control over all this potential. Plus the fact that he played the euphonium, the sax, the trumpet, and he sang a bit as well.

So, there was no shortage of talent, but something, as I say, was still missing.

Whatever that might be.

TEN

Round, Round

We had finished a hard-working sweaty night in the Seapoint Ballroom in Salthill, County Galway and were carrying the gear down the three flights of steel stairs at the side of the hall. It had been a fairly big house and although there was nothing in it for the cobra, things were good.

It was Damien who approached me and said, "Listen to this head, what do you think?"

"Round, round, get around, I get around," and my head blew off. It was the first time I had ever heard the Beach Boys.

This was special and immediately I sensed that this was what we had been waiting for. It sounded like Billy singing the lead, but never before had I heard such falsetto runs and philharmonic sunshine chords, all supported by a deep-throat bass voice, which jumped out of the little recorder. Joy, and then some, with heart-pounding delight. This was altogether different from the Beatles, the Stones and any other band you could care to name. It was enough to waken a need; the need to hear it again. And we must have listened to it for an hour or so on the way home from Galway. It was played over and over again until the batteries went dead. Even today, when I hear it, there is a sense of wonder at its power.

And so was born the Freshmen's great romance with the surf-rock craze that was taking hold on the west coast of the USA. This was a major wake-up call for us and we all rose bright and breezy to its demand and overnight transformed our music, style, clothes, vocabulary, image and direction. This was our destiny. We would become the Irish Beach Boys and people still remember the band for that great copycat ability.

It was also the beginning of the end for the crazy brass section, which had played havoc with my brain. In a short time, Billy would have an electric keyboard and Sean would be playing the trombone and trumpet a lot less, as he was singing the baritone harmony.

We had an ideal blend of voices for a Beach Boys cover band. Billy, on lead vocal, sounded much like either of the singing Wilson brothers, and with Damien's falsetto and Davy's tenor riding my bass and Mahon's baritone, the sound we came up with was exhilarating.

At first it was very strange working out the harmonies, singing and blending them in. We all had to learn new skills. Our musical director took to the task with relish and his arrangements were a challenge. It went like this.

We would play a Beach Boys number, and Bill would allocate each singer his part. When you had run over it a couple of times and were reasonably sure, he would then move onto the next closest harmony to your line. And so on. When all five singers were reasonably confident of their notes, we would stand around the piano and sing out the phrase. More often than not there would be a few bluffers, but it was impossible to get away. Even with five voices belting it out, the leader's ear would call a halt and the offending voice or voices would be re-rehearsed until the wall of harmony rang true. Jaysus, I'll never forget the thrill of singing those early parts.

Then it was time to match voices and instruments and when all hands were happy, we did it through the mikes.

Any harmony singer will attest to the experience of singing a line with another progression which is not the melody. It takes a lot of practice and also the attention to the exact phrasing of the group demands a discipline I had never learned as a solo singer.

Simple things, like starting and ending as one together, are very hard to do. But if they're not there, the thing goes to a total arse. The trick was to avoid what we called "shipwreck endings"; every man for himself. The line of voices had to begin, and end, as one. Tight.

The effort was well worth it and the first time we played in Cork with a couple of Beach Boys songs thrown into the mix, the world began to change. There's an old saying that when Ireland sinks, Cork floats. It was certainly true in our case.

We had a good following in the North, but would have been hard-pressed to come up with even one venue where we could say that we were the numero uno boys. The promoter would always be telling you about how big a crowd Joe, Brendan, Larry, Eileen, Dickie, Prickie or Mickey had done the week before. He downplayed your crowd so as to justify not giving more dough for the return visit, but it was good to hear as it kept a man and a band on its toes. "No stopping" was the cry; we were men on a mission.

We played in Cork a couple of times and, again, scored a few goals, but there was nothing to get excited about. As part of a promotional campaign in the area, the Demp arranged for us to go onstage at the interval of a cinema concert headlined by the Royal Showband. I think our accents had the biggest impact on the ladies that night, and we were marked as "interesting" material to be checked out at a later time.

When we went to the Arcadia in Cork for the next gig, there was a good turnout and it was amazing the effect the Northern twang had on the women. They couldn't believe it and weren't shy about telling us. They weren't shy about anything and were to provide magnificent hospitality over the years. We played three or four Beach Boys hits and the reception was famous. The stage in the Arcadia was halfway up a wall and the band, literally, looked out over the heads of the dancers. You had to look downwards, and they foxtrotted and twisted their night away, right underneath it.

And that wasn't the only thing that happened beneath the bandstand. The autograph-signing session was intense and there was opportunity galore for celebration. She stood so close to the cobra that he began to pant her name and I was more excited by her openness than he was. We gradually edged our way to the back wall, along which ran a row of upright chairs. Cuddling and caressing, nibbling and tonguing, before I knew it the Cobra had slipped out of my opened zipper. Holy Jaysus, this was serious. I had had a couple of drinks, but this was getting dangerous. I was aware of the stories about Satan being seen in such and such a ballroom and had heard all the tales of the women looking down and witnessing her mickey-dancing partner's cloven hoof, but just then, under that stage, there was no stopping him, or indeed, her.

It was passion al fresco, in the ballroom of romance. When the adrenalin is pumping throughout your core, and the sweat is running up your back, and the serpent has been kissed by warm, gently throbbing flesh, it does not take long to convulse. Sweet, sexy, stolen, beautiful and bold, we tongue-kissed our goodbyes where we stood. This was a wild daughter of Ireland; these were the women I had dreamed about. Somebody must have seen us, but there were no sightings of underworld demons reported in the papers the next day. Her "so cool" attitude belied her "so hot" body. I thought about her all the way home and looked forward to our next gig by the Lee. His lordship slept like a baby viper. After we had the gear safely stashed in the wagon, we were treated to crates of beer, bottles of brandy and trays of freshly made sandwiches by the charming Prendergast brothers. These were gentlemen whose company a man could really enjoy. And what better way to prepare for the run back from Cork to Belfast than with a feed of serious drink.

Our next visit down to the Munster capital was to the little port of Crosshaven. We had played it one time before and had an average crowd and equally average reception, but this time it was different.

Gerry Lucey and his brother Murt were the promoters and they told us on arrival that we were going to do a "big un". There were huge numbers of buses coming out from Cork city and it was looking good. Rory Gallagher's band was on first and he also told us that the place would be packed.

That meant it would be hot and that, in turn, meant it would be horny. Heat and a big crowd stuffed together all generated an extra energy up to the stage. When that took off, there would be no stopping it until a frenzy was reached and your head was well on its way to the outer limits of mental distortion. That's how the thing played out onstage, whatever about what was happening on the dance floor. The expectation was added to by a couple of slugs of whiskey in the narrow passageway that served as a dressing room. Rory was building up a heatwave outside and the Freshmen were standing there listening and wondering why such a talent should ever have to play support for anyone.

And then we were on.

There was a scent of danger in the air, and when the curtains pulled back the place went crazy.

Our opening was greeted with row upon row of screaming women. I had never heard nor seen anything like it in my entire life. There were about three thousand people packed into this cauldron of expectancy and about a thousand of them were fighting to get near the stage. Jumping, shouting, waving and crying out our names; it was an amazing scene.

For a moment, I didn't know how to react. But it was just a tiny moment. The adrenalin kicked in and the voice blasted out and all I could see were grabbing, beseeching, outstretched and frantic arms. I began to do my ball-waving routine and this added to the disappearing grasp on reality – theirs and mine. It was fascinating to move close to this sea of outstretched arms and then pull back. I had never done this before. It was something surreal and there was a cock-spell aura of power about the whole glowing mass of bodies screaming your name and urging you to come forward for the touch. Such was the excitement there was no time to think; it was as if the whole thing had been laid on by some massive event planner and everyone was playing a pre-ordained part, but the exact opposite was the case. This was naked impulse, unleashed with a ferocious cacophony of high-pitched female sensuality.

Straight into the second song, with a full band backing and strong harmony on the chorus line. It sounded great up where we were, but it's doubtful if it could be heard halfway down the hall, so great was the din. Brown was standing up in the middle of three brass and hordes of hungry women were trying to touch him. The noise grew and before I knew it, pairs of hands had grasped my legs and groin and I was rolling head first into the throng of dementia surrounding the front of the stage.

Trying to stop my fall with a mike stand, I missed it and was pulled straight down onto the floor and the mike pulled out of my hand. Maurice, knowing the value of a pound, was after it like a bolt of lightning. He grabbed the lead, which was just about to be pulled out of the amplifier, and retrieved it before it could disappear, like the singer, into the frantic crowd. He moved back to his brass position beside Brown and Mahon and continued to blow, leaving me and the serpent at the mercy of the screaming women who, by now, were intent on reaping revenge on the poor excited, hard-as-nails, rockin' reptile. It wasn't clear if they were going to rip it off me for a souvenir or just celebrate his health, but two bouncers pushed to the rescue and humped me back up to the middle of the chaos centre before I found out. What could a man do? I grabbed the skull again and waved the by-now totally confused cobra back down at them. Jaysus, it was mighty *craic*.

When you arrive at the top of the mountain, the natural thing to do is take a rest before you begin the descent. But on this night we seemed to begin at the peak and the excitement just continued to rise. I was empowered by a fearless driving force that told me I could jump through the roof if I wanted to. I felt the bolts of electric thunder-shocks rattle my heart, pound into my head and my screaming voice was the vehicle for this all-powerful, head-wrecking music that drove the women and me wild. I wasn't paying attention to the men, but they were in there somewhere. Looking around at the Freshmen, they seemed to be taking it all in their stride, but I knew it was just an act. They were ignoring the mania out front, or at least, pretending they were. They were just as pumped as me, but not as close to the action.

We had never seen women trying to get onto the

stage before, but by the time we were into the third number the bouncers were at it again. These wild women were serious. Most of them were driven by the heat; the place was packed and there was more room where we stood than there was anywhere else for these steaming, screaming pilgrims. Again, it was unclear what, if anything, they would do if they succeeded in climbing up beside us. I think there must have been a bit of "It's coming from up there somewhere, and I want to get to its core", interlaced with the desire to escape the throng and manic crush. Whatever it was, it didn't cool down.

Our normal routine was to play three or four songs on the bounce and then say a couple of words of introduction. "Hello there, it's good to be back; it's great to be alive," or something fairly bland like that.

But as I tried to speak into the Shure, the words were drowned out and when Billy sat down at the keyboard and Damien played the opening bars of the Chuck Berry-esque guitar riff that was the intro to "Fun, Fun, Fun", our first Beach Boys offering of the night, I thought the fuckin' place would explode. If it had been raucous and wild before, it now reached straitjacket levels of demented fever, and this time the men were playing a competing role with their entranced womenfolk.

Heads shook and rattled; lads jumped up and down and grabbed whoever was standing beside them, in a mixture of dance and grope-fest. We sang our heads off in five-part harmony and the bouncers were now protecting Billy and his fragile keyboard. The ladies were shaking it and pulling and pushing at his mike, which naturally, kept banging into his mouth, a most unpleasant thing when you are sitting down with your hands on the ivories where you can't protect your face. They weren't aware of any of this, of course, but I could see that Mr Brown, although carrying on like a real trooper, was about to stand up and depart for a safer place. He was in danger of losing his teeth.

For the first time in my life as a singer, I really believed that the thing would have to be called off. It was getting out of hand and there didn't seem to be enough minders around to maintain control. It never occurred to me to try and cool the music, to slow the thing down a bit and, anyway, it was Maurice who literally called the tune and the tunes, and he was showing no sign of panic.

For a solid hour it continued like this. There was very little easing of the tension between us and the sea of excitement out front, and as each different singer took the mike to render, the buzz ballooned.

This was where Damien's great gift of being able to identify material from America that would not become mainstream, but if played by us, would make us different from other travelling bands, really came to the fore. Music from the Band and Robbie Robertson, who sometimes backed Bob Dylan, and the early offerings of Canned Heat and the like, were what helped us build a different sound. They were the fillers, but were cool enough to be deemed hip by audiences who were on the lookout for something different.

This wasn't a night to play the Yenka; there was no room to swing around and throw your legs up in the air. There would be plenty of opportunity for that, of course, later, but in this pressure cooker it was not on. It wouldn't have been at home in any case. There was no room in this Mecca of cool that night, for a continental stroll. This was all about drop-top, souped-up, high-revvin', movin'-down-the-highway type of thing. It was a night for revvin' up your Corvette and leaving the Volkswagen Beetle at home. It was all pure escape.

Then it began to subside. It would have been impossible to keep it up for any longer, to sustain this level of passion, and there was a mixture of relief and disappointment when the bedlam ran itself out. It was strange to stand now and smile and nod and wink and confirm the eye seduction in a semi-calm manner. You could hear what the lads were saying to you, and when one of them was singing there was the quick chance of slipping off into the little passageway for a quick shot of the firewater. Maurice frowned upon this, naturally, so you had to say you were taking a leak.

Our programme was geared, like all the bands, to go semi-flat for about forty minutes of the second hour, and then to build to a knockout crescendo of non-stop action for the final twenty. A couple of encores would normally ensue and the job would be done and dusted in about ten extra minutes.

But this special night, we couldn't stop playing for an extra half hour. They demanded it and it was a sign that, wherever else we may or may not hit the big time, we certainly had made the grade in Cork. As I stood feasting my eyes on the luscious ladies who were standing to attention, like the serpent, for the national anthem, my clothes were soaked in sweat. I was drenched. My band outfit would have to be dry-cleaned before being worn again and I couldn't wait to get out of it and into something even hotter.

That night we sported striped jackets with black slacks and blue shirts with white paper collars. Yes, paper collars. They were a tremendous boon to a travelling musician who lived on his own in a Belfast flat. The shirt would last at least a couple of nights and all a fella had to do was put on a brand-new starched collar and no one would be any the wiser.

But like all gimmicks, the paper collars had a serious downside. When the gig got too hot, the sweat would run from the scalp, down your cheeks and onto the papered neck. Meltdown would follow, and before too long a dapper-looking guy would be belting out a lung-threatening, glass-breaking, gut-wrenching rock-chant, with a paper collar hanging down parallel with his tie. Not on.

But on this amazing night, none of that mattered, either to the bemused band of Northern invaders or to the hungry hordes of Munster revellers.

I had a few more swigs of the hard stuff before going back onstage, wearing a dry shirt to autograph the photos, arms and any other body part offered. But the rush at stage front was overwhelming. There was no chance of getting down onto the floor and it took about an hour of this ritual before any serious business could be negotiated. It was still steamy hot and some of the mini-skirted enthusiasts were quite upfront about their plans.

"Can we get a ride back to Cork in the van, Derek?" was the gist of it and as there were more offers than could possibly be entertained, and more men negotiating than myself, there were quite a few refusals. All the while I was casting my eye about for my beautiful encounter in the Arcadia, but she was nowhere to be seen. I was hoping she would show, but if she did she hadn't deemed it worth the wait, or more likely, her need that night wouldn't permit any delay in celebrating the great imperious urge.

It took a bit of banter with a righteous night porter at the door of the Metropole Hotel to get the girls in. He muttered something about having to be residents, but the gay crowd just swarmed past him. Perhaps he didn't have any moral objections about this band of excited Nordies and their hungry entourage, but I think he envisaged a long few hours of work ahead as soon as it reached the residents' lounge up on the first floor. He would be carrying drink, as the man says, to beat the band; to beat them into bed and out of his nice, clean comfort zone. It was about half four in the morning.

Not all of the band partook of the harvest, but I was in there following the serpent, as he confused his over-enthusiastic head about where to settle for the night. The *craic* was mighty and the drink was flowing, and it seemed a shame to have to make a choice at all.

This was paradise. I had one lovely companion ready to rock, but it was hard to focus on just having one roll. The adrenalin pump hadn't switched off yet and it was as if all I wanted was to keep the whole vibe going. I didn't want it to stop and the whiskey was driving it on.

I was thinking to myself that the proper thing to do would be for us all to strip down, right there in the residents' lounge, and move on to a higher sexual plane. We would all be available to all comers. That would have been better, I imagined, than just having to settle for a one-off, but that fantasy was not to materialise that night. I used to read in school about the wonders of ancient Rome and their great fondness for stuff like this, and I was thinking they weren't far wide of the mark. The energy died before this marvel could happen. I have a feeling that the amount of drink I had on board had something to do with it.

There was something else going on in that Cork hotel, something that would present itself as a growing problem in the future. I once wrote a song, "Big Skins", and it was about a lad who couldn't get enough of anything.

> His "I've had enough switch" was broken at
>   birth
> There was no stoppin' his drinkin' or singin'
> The bottles were clinkin', his brain was
>   shrinkin'
> Because of the booze and the *craic* and the
>   women.

That desire for more of everything, that merciless greed for extra helpings of whatever instant pleasure was at hand, that driving impulse for higher, louder, sexier, stronger, was an indication that the "switch" was dangerously faulty. I didn't see it at the time.

Communal sex or not, that night was something that every man should experience once in his life and it marked out the village of Crosshaven and the Majorca ballroom as a special place, the Fire Palace of Ireland.

A few hours earlier there had been a blue energy all around the stage; the steam was rising and you know what that means. Everything was rising and wouldn't go down for a decade or so. The phrase "by popular demand", had taken on a whole new meaning; this night showed me its meaning, and it was destined to continue.

One of the lines from "I Get Around" goes:

> My buddies and me are getting real well known

and the proof of it was right before our excited eyes.

This was more like it. We had it made. In Cork, we were the men. Freshmen.

ELEVEN

I'm Young, I'm Young

We took the passion wagon over to England on the boat and headed off on the first English tour as Derek Dean and the Freshmen. The lads had done it all before, but it was my introduction to singing outside the local scene.

"Tour" is an interesting word. Our life at home was an everlasting tour by now, but no one ever called it that. We were working six or seven days and nights a week, covering thousands of miles, but we never imagined it as a tour. It was the job, a wonderful occupation and one you would never exchange for any other, but it was still work. The word "tour" seemed to imply that we had other business and every so often we would leave that to begin travelling around the country for a defined period of time.

But this sortie to England was the real deal for

me.

Whereas the Six of One had worked the top-rank circuit, which involved mainly English audiences, this venture was to centre on the Irish venues in the likes of Birmingham, Manchester and London. It was during Lent, the down time for entertainment in the Republic, and was a diversion from the non-stop action at home. The crowds were good but, not surprisingly, the reception wasn't anything like the rave reactions we had been getting in Cork and, increasingly, in other places as well.

Nevertheless, we did the biz in the North and the Midlands and headed down the M1 to the big smoke. I couldn't wait to sing in London and had always had a ball when I'd been there before.

As a lad of 17, I'd gone with a mate from college in Belfast to work for the summer holidays in Blackpool as a tram conductor, and, on the day we left, we managed to derail one of them in Manchester Square, the busiest intersection in the Lancashire seaside resort. Consequently, when we went back the following year, the town's transportation authority decided they could do without our specific talents and so we headed on a bus down to London, eager to sample its delights.

We arrived in the city at 2 p.m. and were in a strip club by 4 p.m. You see, in those days, there were no strippers in the northern-English holiday capital, at least none that we could find. And there were certainly none that any man could find in Ireland – North or South.

My brother Gerry met us at the terminus and, railing against our mission, grudgingly went with us on this much-anticipated quest. But it was to prove to be a major disappointment. Seedy and greedy, it was a rip-off beyond belief and the women were, shall I say, past their prime.

The rest of that summer was a mixture of falling in love with a divorced young Cockney mother, and singing, dancing, listening to the chart shows and doing the very odd bit of work, making steel frames for concrete pipes. I loved London and imagined the upcoming gigs would be something special.

But the experience in the capital's ballrooms was not so enjoyable. With a few notable exceptions, the kind of people who were going to the shows were second cousins to the disinterested dancers in Borris-in-Ossory. The halls in London had been a meeting place for emigrants for decades and, in that environment, the music stayed rooted, in their minds and eyes, somewhere back in 1953. It was a very simple, beautiful and profitable bit of nostalgia; a homesick reverie with musical accompaniment.

They wanted to hear what they had left behind; yer man with the fartin' fiddle and his mate on a placid piano, cranking out a backing over which ballads about a bitter deal in life could be keened. And they hadn't invited us band of intruders, with our ultra-loud, in-your-face, rock 'n' cock version of modern Ireland.

We were something of an annoyance to them and their sexual appetite seemed to be as hidden as it had been on the day of their departure from the land of saints and scholars.

The Demp put the tour together and he didn't seem to care. In hindsight, it probably wasn't the greatest example of successful product placement in the showband circuit, but the Demp had other fish to fry. He wanted to get the band heard in England and it was a lot easier to take record company execs to a venue in London than it was to take them to Belfast. It was work, after all, when there was none in Ireland. So, on with it.

The hotel we stayed in was in Bayswater and was owned by a couple of lads from the west of Ireland who had done very well for themselves. We had a roadie by this stage, and he and I were sitting around for a couple of hours, sipping hard liquor. It was early in the afternoon and that night we were due to play in New Cross. The magic idea struck me that we needed a bit of adventure to brighten things up.

"Ever been to a brothel, Jack?"

"Be the holy, no, but I'd love to," was the earnest reply.

As more and more whiskey disappeared down his big frame, the thoughts of a lightening encounter with real-life London prostitutes (the term hooker wasn't then in vogue) became more and more attractive.

"Do you think we should?" was his slurred query about an hour later. The thought was obviously driving his head a little horny.

"We'll give it a bit more time yet, they may not be open," was my innocent response. I imagined they must have some kind of opening hours and maybe three o'clock was a bit too early for these magnificent women.

By now the drink was having an obvious effect. I took some more and stood up from the table and went over to the porter, who sported a shock of red hair that would have enraged a senile bull.

"Have you any idea where a man could find a

knocking shop around here?"

He looked at me with pure disgust. He was horrified that a good Catholic Irish boy, as he assumed we all were, should want to visit such a den of ill repute and sin, glorious sin. One of the lads, a day or so earlier, had told me that this particular individual was a failed priest. He had either been found wanting in the spiritual department or had just missed out on his exams, but either way this was some angry man in front of me. His face matched the colour of his hair, as he practically had a fit at the idea.

"You should be ashamed of yourself, talking like that; you're nothing but a disgrace to your country."

"Aw, go fuck yourself, and then fuck a brasser and then have a good wank at the thought of it," or words to that effect was all I could say to him. And I began to elaborate in detail what I intended to do when I finally got my wicked way. I was a bit intoxicated, for sure, but I genuinely couldn't see the harm in paying your dues to working women, women of the afternoon.

He continued to rant and rattle on about God and the Devil and how I was representing the lower division and letting Mother Macree down in the most scandalous manner.

At that moment a celebrated actor from a TV series came in the door with a big, shiny, painted-to-the-nines loveboat – a lady to die for. He had played a role in the cop show *Softly, Softly* and was a well-recognised face. All I could do was laugh and when he looked over at this big, drunk, giggling Paddy, I congratulated him on his good fortune and asked him where a lad could find a happy House of Sin in the area.

"Ask him, mate," he said, pointing to the taxi-driver outside the hotel doors, counting his change in the cab.

"Come on Jack, hurry up, we're on," I roared, and when I hurried past the Raging Redhead on the way out, I repeated in spurts what I intended to do once I had been afforded the occasion. He looked on aghast and screwed up his face in pain at the graphic nature of it all. It was frantic.

"Can you take us to a kipshop mister, somewhere not too expensive, and not too big a rip-off?"

"Get in," he said, and off he headed with his two drunken tourists in the back, laughing hysterically.

Suddenly we stopped and the taxi-man said: "It's a good shop, I use it myself. Just knock on that door there and you'll be fine."

Two lecherous and slightly unsteady cocks waited at the portal to the Promised Land. I had assured the roadie that the treat was on me and that I would cover all expenses, and when the door opened I was glad I had.

She covered the entire frame; you couldn't see past her. She was a massive lady and I thought for sure that she was the bouncer, the receptionist or something, but couldn't imagine she was on for business. I, and I'm sure Jack as well, had envisaged a slender, sensuous, pouting wet-feast of a Cockney nymphette who spent her days lusting after randy Irishmen.

"Is this er, er, a … you know?"

"It is, come in. I'll take one of you and the other can go upstairs to that door up there on the right.

You pay first and there are no refunds. It's a fiver each. OK?"

I was nearly hysterical and was afraid I'd burst out laughing at any second. It was my treat, so Jack was her man and I would take my luck upstairs. Before she took my smiling mate into the downstairs closet, I handed over the tenner and asked if there was any drink in the house.

"Later," was all she said.

Sobering up a good bit, I headed up the stairs and approached the door. The serpent had reared his beautiful head by now and was anticipation incarnate. He stiffened my resolve.

The portal of wild promise swung open and the voice merely said, "Come in."

Upon entering the tiny bedroom, I saw immediately why she hadn't come out to greet me. She couldn't. This was the biggest human being I had ever seen. There was no shape at all. Just a moving, talking, mini-marquee of flesh and bone with an ability to utter human-like sounds. Jack's was like Twiggy compared to this squeaking jelly-cat and I was now cursing myself for being such an idiot. I should have been less selfish and made friends with the receptionist.

"Take your cock out mate and I'll wash it in the sink before we start," she croaked in a strained, Cockney accent.

I was afraid of her and didn't know what to do. I thought about running out and making a safe escape, but I wasn't too sure. It was like standing in front of a sci-fi monster that is moving slowly in your direction. If she jumped on me, I'd be dead for sure, I would smother. I really wanted to run and I don't know what stopped me. The brain was reacting slowly or maybe it was the sheer devilment of it all that kept me on the edge. I thought to myself that there was no way out for the poor woman, or indeed, me. She couldn't, physically, and I couldn't, cowardly.

Anyway, the lumbering Lothario was now fumbling at the serpent's zipper and he made the shyest entrance I had ever, ever, experienced. He was like a soft, over-ripe banana and didn't come alive until she rubbed the warm, soapy water down into the only eye he had, at the top of his head. The whole thing took on an air of complete dementia when she began to sing to herself. Holy Jaysus. I began to fret about crazy, knife-wielding eunuch makers, but things took a turn for the better when the serpent decided to rise to the occasion. It must have been his reaction to her warbling, but it didn't matter now. It was a truly amazing feat and I followed him as he followed her slowly across the room to the tiny bed in the corner.

As she lowered herself gently and with great skill onto the mattress, I watched in disbelief as she pulled up her wigwam size dress and struggled to part two massive, nylon-clad, tree-trunk thighs. I was too afraid to look and see if she was wearing suspenders, as I had imagined a fallen woman should, but there was no denying this was a game warrior I had encountered. There were no eyes that I could make out in the rounds of flesh that made up her face, so I wasn't sure if she was chuckling now, crying or panting. In all fairness to this working woman, she grunted and shunted her arse until she got the enormous legs wide enough for me to lie down between them.

I was expecting the bed to collapse and thought that if I were to get on top, then its legs would crumble. But they didn't and pretty soon the place was rolling. It was something like a ride on a choppy sea, and I imagined that surfing must be something akin to this. Maybe this was what they meant by "riding the wave". There was a minor danger of suffocation as I disappeared into the mounds of enormous, creamy flesh, but this fear departed as soon as the cobra found his way into the rented promised land.

"I'll just lie here for a bit; let yourself out."

It was over and I wasn't too sure how I felt – exhilarated or depressed – but one thing I knew for certain. I needed a drink, so I hurried downstairs. The earlier stuff was dying and the noise from a downstairs room led me into a happy scene where Jack and his mot were enjoying a few drinks. He looked like a happy man and was reasonably sober, although his intentions were clear as he was holding a fairly stiff glass of something or other in his fist.

"You got on OK, Paddy?" the first heavyweight smiled.

"I got on," was all I came back with. "Can I have a drink?"

She brought sustenance to the table, which was in front of a roaring fire, and the session began all over again.

"What was yours like?" asked a still-grinning Jack.

"Mighty, mighty," was all I could say. It would be too dangerous to start, and you never knew who might be about.

We were well into our third or fourth drink

and the sated roadie had mentioned a couple of times that perhaps we should be on our way back to the hotel, when a vision appeared. A stunning blonde, waist-length hair flowing down her back, an everything-you-ever-dreamed-of bombshell, walked straight in front of us from another room and she was completely stark naked. She just casually strolled past us and, as I stood up to follow, the lady of the house pulled me back down.

"She's not available," was all she would say to my stuttering, urgent pleas for service.

"She doesn't work here."

Sometime soon after this apparition, we asked the Madame if she could call us a taxi. We finished the drink in front of us and next thing we were travelling in the black cab back to Bayswater. The driver was a soft-spoken, tweed-capped, fair-haired man who assured us that he knew the beautiful blonde in the brothel.

I was still desperately trying to find out about this sex goddess, but the driver assured me that, unlike the flabby floozy, she wasn't a pro but was a "special person" who just happened to live there.

Confused and slightly disoriented by now, I was still trying to work it all out, when two things happened that seemed like a nightmare to my brain. Jack was drooling on about some mad scheme to open a good whorehouse in Kildare, when the bizarre became real.

There was a group of would-be passengers outside the hotel trying to hail a cab and, looking out, I thought they looked vaguely familiar. As I turned to pay the driver, he took off his cap, unfurled his hair, and all at once, he had become she. This was the naked blonde. I thought I was really going crazy, but turned to see a very angry man knocking at the back window and shouting profanities in at the now totally perplexed and bewildered roadie and myself. It was Maurice and the rest of the boys who had just been thrown out of the righteous hotel. Their entire luggage at their feet, they stood there in disgust, howling loud, angry words, which were far from complimentary to the pair of us.

I thought Maurice might break the window, and roared at the androgynous cabbie to get moving. But she insisted we get out. If she hadn't, who knows where the whole thing might have ended? As it was, I helped Jack, the intended Kildare sin-spreader, out of the back of the chariot and straight into some serious bollickin' from the lads. I was trying to tell them the *craic*, but they were too annoyed to listen.

"Fuck you, Bigman," was the general chorus.

The wannabe, but couldn't be, priest, had gone to the two hotel owners and insisted that the dirty band of Northern sinners be barred from the hotel. Not just me, but the whole ensemble. When the lads had arrived back at the digs after an afternoon sampling other, more mundane, delights of London, they were given their marching orders. And they were told why by the revenging redneck. I have a feeling that perhaps this frustrated man was harbouring deep grudges against his Northern brothers. He had the air of a man of war and this opportunity was a real boon to his bile.

I don't remember much about the gig that night, nor where, if anywhere, I stayed. I never even went back to the hotel to get my gear. I was in the doghouse for a couple of days and every second sentence I said was "I'm sorry". But Brown and Mahon loved the story. Jack sobered up and was on his best behaviour for the remainder of the tour. I don't think he ever got around to opening the knocking shop, but on that day he was full of great ambition.

I had never seen such beauty as that displayed by the naked taxi-driver. She was a dream and was destined to remain so in my head. Maybe it was Beauty-and-the-Beast syndrome, having gone from one extreme to another in the same building. Or perhaps it was a bottle-and-a-half-of-whiskey syndrome. But whatever else it was, it was truly unforgettable.

In time, the English circuit became as familiar as the one at home and we craved the opportunity to work in front of a younger, challenging audience. Sometimes we would visit Scotland in our travels and some of the Antrim brethren got to listen to the unadulterated version of their mother tongue.

So we were thrilled at the idea of playing at a students' end-of-year party in Manchester University along with Blodwyn Pig, an underground British hardcore four-piece. It was a two-band show and, like all such events, it turned into a battle of the bands. The Pig were formed by blues guitarist Mike Abrahams who had played with Jethro Tull, but the main man in the blues/rock show was a sax player by the name of Jack Lancaster.

They were, like ourselves, very loud, and built up a head of steam with synchronised riffs and intricate tempo changes, but when big Jack blew a solo the place really jumped, or shall I say bounced. You see, instead of smashing his guitar over the amplifier *à la* Hendrix and Townsend, he bounced himself off the floor. How he did it was an art known only to himself, but I swear he would blow up a head of steam and then, in the middle of the screeching wail, throw himself and the horn down onto the boards. Without stopping or wrecking the tenor, he'd jump right back up and drive her on round the bend.

So, on that particular night, with the students all agog and loving every minute of it, the Freshmen had to play up or pipe down. It was a marvellous gig and, in the end, I think even honours were declared.

There was a decent bit of booze shared as well. What else would you expect and we found ourselves back at the hotel, shall we say, well oiled.

Earlier that afternoon I had looked on in great admiration as a real English stunner walked into the reception area accompanied by what looked like her grandparents. She had everything in all the right places and her shyness to the stare made her even more attractive. The three disappeared to their accommodation, but a couple of the brethren were hoping it wouldn't be long until we'd see them, or at least her, again.

The moment passed and we headed off to the college to set up and do a sound check and now, standing rather unsteadily, pulling down the arm of a stubborn slot machine, I was lost in a world of my own. There had been a brief encounter with a young enthusiast after the gig, but for one reason or another she hadn't made it back to the hotel.

Pulling on the losing handle one more time, I blearily watched the slots whirl around when, from the side, a groping hand encircled the slumbering beast, which stood straight to attention.

"Hit the jackpot yet?"

It was the granny. It was the honey's mother's mother. Oh Jaysus, I thought, this is wild.

"No, but it looks like I'm about to," was my initial response and the trouser leg was swelling in anticipation. "Where's your granddaughter, is she anywhere about?"

She assured me that a great night lay in store, and all I had to do was follow her to her room, and see to her needs and then you'd never know what might happen. She repeated her room number and was gone. I hadn't asked her if grandpa was under the sheets, but I didn't really care. There was adventure in the air, and as I watched her leave the bar it must have been about half three in the morning.

Some of the lads were finishing up for the night, and I couldn't wait to tell them of my mission.

They didn't believe it and fell about laughing, so I invited them to come up and listen in. I began to get thick with their disbelief and swallowed another couple of shots before ascending the stairs, assuring them of greater conquests in store. I was boasting that, after her, it was all arranged that I would be fixed up for Heaven, and a giggling band of drunken musicians chaperoned me to her door. We were all in a state of delirious expectation, none more so than the serpent, who burst in the door, leading the way to perdition.

I couldn't have been more than 23 or 24 at the time, but she was touching 70. As she stood in her baby-doll nightie, glass of brandy in extended hand, and smiling the wrinkliest smile I'd ever seen, my first instinct was to run. I think it was the big glass of napper that swung the decision because, truth to tell, the reptile was about to baulk for the first time in its hungry life.

I could hear the lads outside the door and there were a few yahoos, which I thought wasn't quite in keeping with the solemnity of the occasion. It was different inside the door than outside. In here it was deadly serious stuff. I milled the warm liquid and she pulled back the covers and lay down on the bed, welcoming me on board.

"Aw, fuck it, give it a go," I thought and lay down on top, struggling not to kill her. I didn't know how strong she was and if she could take it – the weight I mean – but take it she could. My drunken head was thinking about the escapade in the brothel, but I ignored it. The serpent slid into granny's grotto, and she began to squeal at the top of her voice.

The boys at the door were howling with glee, and I caught the insanity.

She screamed at the top of her fading lungs, "Great ... facking great ... facking great!" in a cultured but frenetic English accent.

All my demented head could come out with was, 'I'm Young, I'm Young'.

And the lads outside nearly fell through the door.

I came to consciousness about two hours later. The tongue was swollen in my mouth, and it was dry like a desert bone as my eyes opened to the strange ceiling. I knew I wasn't in Belfast, for I didn't recognise the decor, and I was about to raise my head from the pillow when I felt the warm body beside me.

I slowly turned my pounding skull to look and was horrified at what greeted my half-opened, guilty eyes. Granny was sound asleep on her side of the bed, faced towards me. She had removed her teeth sometime before she went asleep and now her jawline was sucked right in as she exhaled little expulsions of syncopated breath from her tiny perch-like mouth.

Spotting the glass of brandy of a few hours earlier on the dressing table, I slid out of the deathbed, hoping there would be some left. But, alas, I had drained it all. My stomach was dry-retching as I raised the glass to my mouth, but it wasn't just the smell of the liquor that had me shattered. Even though my chest was heaving, I tried to stick my enlarged licker down the inside of the glass in my body's begging attempt for liquid.

I dressed and, as I left the chamber, I couldn't help but feel that old Mr Karma was up there somewhere making notes in his ledger. Mr Freshman was running up a big debt. It was He who reputedly wrote the law that says responsibility for "unskilful" actions is borne by the person who commits them, and I was building up a mighty store of "hell-to-pay" nights; I'm sure you know what I'm talking about.

But "I'm Young, I'm Young" became a rallying cry. Whenever things got down, with a dance dragging on for a lifetime, with not much happening upstage, someone would crack the words and merriment would be restored. It was a powerful mindset for the business we were in.

TWELVE

Go West Young Men

When we returned from one of these mad escapades, the press release always spoke of how the band took such and such a place by storm. We had a contract of sorts, as I already mentioned, with Pentagon Promotions in Shaftesbury Square and we weren't short-changed by their proffered piffle. The whole thing was well organised and the fan club had a growing base.

"What about a trip to the States, Bigman?" were the magic words that came dropping from the Demp's wonderful lips. I had never been asked such an exciting question. "We're going out for three weeks and are booked for New York, Boston and Chicago."

This was beyond my wildest dreams. I loved Belfast, adored Dublin, venerated London and its holy shrines, but New York?

"Ah Jaysus, Peter, you're kiddin' me," was my hopeful reply.

"No, sir, it's all arranged. There's a bit involved at this end, with visas and injections and passports, but we leave in June."

Of course, Pentagon had it in all the papers. The Freshmen were off to America, to score big goals and make dollar fortunes. Never mind that every band worth the name had done it before us; that wasn't important. We would take it by storm. I determined that although we were going to perform in Irish clubs, the patrons would be of a much more sophisticated variety. After all, they were living in America, the coolest place on the planet. It never occurred to me that those living in London, those who were stuck in "come all ye" Heaven, were also breathing the air of rebellion and change in the 1960s rock capital and it hadn't made any difference.

The Clippers were the first band I knew to travel to the States, and they had been gigging there for so long that the first time they travelled they went by boat. I had heard wonderful tales of adventure and free love from other musicians who had worked the circuit, but most of all I had my wild imaginings. I was dying just to see a yellow taxi and catch a glimpse of a skyscraper, and I couldn't wait to court a real American woman.

"You know you'll have to play a bit of black puddin' over there lads," was the ominous brief from our much-admired manager.

"They have a very strong love for the old country and will be expectin' a few songs their parents taught them."

Oh Holy Jaysus, I thought, and was joined by the

rest of the band in a mini-rebellion.

"No way head, spare us that crap; they have to hear something modern, sure they're Yanks," was our argument. But, in mortal fear of missing the boat, or plane, we relented.

Looking back on it, the sad thing was that a band of Ulstermen should have ignored the great lore of Irish traditional music. We often spoke about originality in this field, but we never acted. Phil Lynott and "Whiskey in the Jar" is a good reminder of what we missed.

We rehearsed a couple of ballads and, in fact, did a rock version of the old Antrim classic "Roddy McCorley". But like most compromises, it was a half-hearted effort and the brethren just weren't interested. Besides, I had the feeling that the sentiment of this particular ditty was not to some of their liking.

Like the Cobra, I was looking forward to this great adventure and couldn't wait to see and sample the American women; a species that had been celebrated in love ballads, rock anthems, magazines and every outlet possible. What were they going to be like? Jaysus, after Grafton Street in Dublin, Royal Avenue in Belfast and Carnaby Street in London, the anticipation was trouser-stretching. I was in a tailspin over the majestic sexual magnetism of the women on my travels so far, but in America, the home of rock 'n' roll, it was sure to be something else. Just what, I couldn't envisage, but hopes were at an all-time high.

Again, this was an example of the "I've had enough switch" being faulty. I never once considered that there was a limit to the amount of pleasure any one man could have. I believed in the vertical ascendancy law; it just went up and up in an inexorable climb to somewhere beyond the clouds and, when it got there, it kept on climbing.

The women in Belfast were beyond any man's dream. They had a natural beauty of line that bore testament to the finest of breeding. This was the result of a sex drive propelled by the cold Lagan air. In other words, their Das and Mas couldn't wait to jump into love after a freezin' night out. They were of the no-car generation, there wasn't enough dough for a taxi, and the buses didn't run late, so you had to walk home after a night out and one thing led to another. The gorgeous ladies of the Sixties came about as the result. These beautiful Ulster sex goddesses wore their mini-skirts high. They saw what was going down in Carnaby Street and weren't going to be surpassed by higher hems sported by their London sisters. It was a truly magnificent era for a young, lean, hungry cocksman. It got better and better on every corner. Walking down any street, lane, or avenue in Belfast city centre was a stroll into dreamland for the reptile and me.

Their skin was so pure. It seemed as if they all had been passed through a delivery system that produced this silken, sylphlike splendour. They seemed untouchable, but they were just the opposite. They too, were out on an adventure of discovery; they too had the spirit of revolution that was in the air, and, in fact, they were leading it.

And what the Lagan ladies had, their Dublin counterparts had in abundance. The same beautiful bounty, the seemingly endless supply of fully ripe, sensuous honey, was everywhere to behold. And getting hold of them was the main reason for being. They had an added bonus: their accents. The way a woman sounds is, for many seekers, the golden key to joy. A different accent than your own is a big turn-on and guaranteed to add a preference into the decision-making process, when all other things are equal. It's the same for both sexes, but in those steamy days the Southern melodic tones were a powerful added attraction.

Much more so than in Belfast, the Dublin ladies represented a greater share of the nation's finest females. There seemed to be a broader migration from all points of the compass and, with the new arrivals, there was a sense of liberation, a freedom from the small-town suffocation these unfulfilled women had known. They would set about changing all that and there was no shortage of menfolk willing to help them right such a woeful wrong.

In its aesthetic sense, there was no beauty to match a pure-bred Dublinette. She attained the highest peaks of perfection and retained the ability to disturb the faculties of even the most balanced of boys and men. This beauty exuded a class all her own; unmatched, unrivalled, thrilling to be near. She spoke with a laughing lilt and challenged you to dare. She was the snake charmer par excellence and the wriggling beast could never ignore her spell. Her magnificence had survived the liquid maelstrom of drunken nights' passion, brought on, in many cases, by the dark aphrodisiac brewed in James's Street and a great many of their number were, undoubtedly, a direct result of a black beer-boogie night, but it didn't in any way detract from their sheer "Oh Holy Jesus, I want to sleep with that woman" aura.

Even in those days the whole world lived in London. Whereas in Belfast and Dublin there was a 99 per cent Caucasian Irish harvest, in the land of the Thames there was a more international flavour to the feast; a veritable cornucopia of the good stuff. If variety is the spice of life, then this town offered a real strong curry. Black, Asian, German, Italian, Swedish and all points European and Australian, lightly-clad ladies strolled its promenades. Any day in Regent Street was enough to send the serpent into a sin-spin and a man's mind wouldn't be straightened out until he had gained some relief, from whatever quarter.

So, if this was the scene over here, what was it going to be like over there?

The anointed day was approaching fast and after what seemed like an eternity of waiting for visas to materialise and a couple of injections against smallpox and every other kind of pox the American government feared might be imported to their homeland by a gang of rabid Paddies, I found myself at Shannon airport, ordering six bottles of Jack Daniel's whiskey, which was my duty-free allowance. Let the games begin.

Our first transatlantic flight was diverted to Montreal for some reason or other and we struck up a session in the arrivals lounge as we awaited our fate. The mini-concert had attracted a decent crowd of pissed-off travellers who seemed most appreciative of this impromptu performance. It was Freshmen "unplugged" for the first time and it soon became obvious that there was one young blonde trekker who wasn't too disappointed by the rescheduling of her trip to the Big Apple.

Hearts dropped when it was announced we

would be over-nighting in a ski lodge an hour's journey from the airport, but I sat beside this Canadian beauty for the bus trip. She had been to Ireland on holiday, but worked in New York and was being met at the airport by her boyfriend. He hadn't been able to make the trip with her because of his job as a cop; he drove a car in the city.

I pondered this for a moment, but it wasn't a long ponder. We had a couple of drinks in the bar of the lodge and, as there was no sign of any blue and whites in the vicinity of this Canadian outpost, headed off to settle in for the night. It was a beautiful beginning to our North-American adventure and was a promising portent of great things to come.

Driving from Kennedy airport in a convertible Mustang, I couldn't believe my eyes. It was the most awe-inspiring sight I had ever seen, and looking at the Manhattan skyline that afternoon is a memory I shall take to my grave. The driver was playing the radio and listening to the jingles and accent of the presenter with its unmistakable "This is America" sound, I believed I really had it made. And I had. You hear that sound everywhere nowadays, but back then it was the first time for me. Today every radio station works to the same formula, which was fresh in those days; sexy jingles, super cool-dude presenter and snappy introductions to high-powered music.

What else could a lad from Strabane ever possibly want? Jaysus, here is where the whole thing was born, where it all was happening; this was the Big Apple, in the flesh and in the concrete. This was the high point of my life. It just kept getting better and better.

Skyscrapers galore, lines of yellow taxis, all

blowing their horns, and motorcars as long as a small train. All shapes and sizes; they were magnificent to behold and they seemed to get bigger by the Avenue. We were staying in the Woodward Hotel in downtown Manhattan and as I lifted the six bottles of Jack Daniel's onto the dresser in my room, manic excitement was tap-dancing at the back of my head. How could I take it all in? Where was the best place to start? When was the kick-off? I took a couple of slugs of the whiskey and breathed deep. The clock was ticking.

I remember the promoter, Dan Kiely, telling the restaurateur that Irish guys didn't like coleslaw. Seems stupid now, but that sticks in my brain. Dan was a millionaire Kerryman who had the knack of turning many dollars in this hub of Irishness. He ran the dances in a couple of venues and seemed to be the main player in the New York-Irish club scene. He had a partner but his was the driving energy that got, and kept, the show on the road. He took no prisoners and when he spoke, others listened.

This son of Kerry showed us the sights of the city and had organised everything for us prior to our arrival; a bus for the gear and transport to and from the gigs. We were only working on Friday, Saturday and Sunday nights, with the rest of the time off for good behaviour. There were a couple of sessions with an Irish radio station, and it was all very relaxed indeed.

Our first couple of days were spent in a semi-daze. The sights, sounds and smells of this hotspot were so different from any other and what was on offer – the food, the buskers, the peep-shows, the three-card trickmen in Times Square, Times Square itself, Fifth Avenue, Gilly's bar and the rest – lit a fire in my heart. I loved it all.

With one major exception.

The first time I walked down a Manhattan street, I thought I must be in the wrong town. I kept looking for them but they were nowhere to be seen. I stared into shops, gazed at all passers-by and poked my head into several restaurants, of which there seemed to be thousands, but I searched in vain.

I was looking for talent, for women; sexy women, women in mini-skirts so short you could trace their thighs to the curve of their hips, and then, mentally, follow that track to Heaven; ladies who would force your head to turn, to wish, to desire and who would reinforce the feeling that it was great to be alive.

But they didn't appear. I didn't see one really horny lady in all of New York City in the couple of days leading up to our first gig. The other men agreed that this was, indeed, the case and that while the eastern seaboard metropolis was a mighty and marvellous place, its womenfolk were a major disappointment, by home standards at least.

There was no fashion, no style, no beautiful attraction, and definitely no sex appeal. Not in the super abundance we had become used to, at any rate. They just didn't have the class of their European competitors. They didn't have the mini either.

It wasn't just the look of this town's womanhood, but their attitude that was a turn-off. They made it clear, right at the start of a conversation, that a man's status was the important thing. How much a man earned decided if the juice would flow or not and if the current could be turned on. And most of them had unhealthy skin. It must have been the hard work schedules they demanded from themselves and a poor diet, but they were a fairly unattractive class of being. I often wondered if this had anything to do with the number of wars that American men found themselves in – that they would prefer to be overseas than at home – but dismissed it as being too improbable a cause. But you never know.

New York was about two years behind London, in the female stakes at least, but it was still a mind-blowing place. And when you speak in general terms about the overall picture, there can be a tendency to overlook its exceptions, its very sexy exceptions. And there were some.

The gigs in the Irish clubs were anticipated with great excitement. We had to play two sets of an hour each instead of doing our usual two-hour stint and this, by its nature, sharpened the band up in a big way. There was no down time in this arrangement, no cooling-off period. You had to begin with a bang and slowly build the show until, approaching the hour mark, all hell would let loose.

A major difference between the clubs in "Noo Yoik" and home was the presence of a drinks licence. People would congregate around the bar area as that's where the night's action was all planned. It was a totally different scene. No charge of the hungry dicks here, just a skilful eyeing-up of the targets and making the initial approach before the booze began to overflow. There was no danger of these women not being accepted in the heart of the action. They were calling for drinks I'd only heard of in the movies, and this added an exotic air to the whole affair. Bourbon, rye, tequila, pina coladas and daiquiri cocktails were ordered with impunity. The ladies may not have been wearing skimpy minis, but they sure knew how to order a drink. This, I thought, was real sophistication; the essence of cool. I never considered that the drinks were just ordinary head-wreckers, no different from the equally exotic stuff we fill the Yanks with when they come to our shores.

After the first set we would head down to the drinks area to scout out the possibility of any loose women, that is, those without a partner. It was important to establish if the smile flashed up during a song was maybe an invitation to something more interesting later on, and to, as the Demp would have cautioned, mix and mingle.

Mostly the dancers had all been born Stateside and were Irish by culture. Their parent's grandparents had set up home in the States, but had never left the oul sod in their heads. They were greener than the Glens of Antrim and took their Irishness very seriously, with most having a very faint idea of what the 1960s Holy Land was actually like. Listening to them talk after the gig, it became clear that, in the main, their vision of Ireland was one of shortage, hardship, backwardness, oppression, holy priests, singing nuns and barefoot, begging children. Now and again you would hear vague, half-drunken talk about freedom for the people from British oppression and that their Irishness would best be served by a "free" Ireland, but apart from kicking out the bad Brits, there was no masterplan of how this free land would actually work. The bar-room thinking of the day was fairly basic. Get shot of Lizzie Windsor's boys and the economic miracle would immediately follow. It would be a natural consequence.

The reality of it was that their emigrant ancestors

had generally been from the rural areas of Ireland and most of them would never, in all probability, have even been on a day trip to Dublin or Belfast. Their plight, real and personal, was only relieved by insufferable agony in uprooting and voyaging to the new land and taking their broken-hearted spirits with them. They had heard that there wasn't much happening in the major towns, so they were forced to find a way out.

They did indeed escape, at an enormous cost to their birthright; a cost they would pay until their death in America. Their children were handed down the Penal Laws paradigm and taught their own children that the money sent home was badly needed, as indeed it was. Individual immigrants would tell sad stories of things not changing in the homeland and woe would follow woe.

The mass communications era was just beginning and transatlantic flight was still a bit of an adventure. There was no Irish TV they could tune into of an evening and no digital preferences, of up to 500 stations from all corners of the globe. Their image of Ireland was a sacred one; a special place where the people were good, holy and simple. There was little sin in this mental imagining, nor indeed, could there be. This was your mother you were pining for, Mother Ireland; pure as the driven snow and as cold as winter.

But they showed a true Irish passion for the *craic*. They were happy enough to have lots of sinning in America and that was something we could all agree on. Hard-working and hard-playing, they really knew how to party at the weekend. The music was an intrusion to them, at times, but you had to dance to something. A big, loud, thundering showband was not what they wanted to hear, but we were Irish, so they would put up with us as long as we played enough slow songs for them to get about the real business.

We didn't make any great waves in the Irish clubs in NY City, but we didn't blow it either. We tried our best to tone it down, but it was a different band when the pedal came off the pulse and we didn't keep it on the edge. Two shows a night really brought a man into the bi-polar realm, but I enjoyed every minute of it.

Mainly it was couples that paid to see the big bands from their motherland and one major difference from the scene in Ireland was the admission price they were willing to pay. About ten times more expensive, but they didn't appear to have any problem with that.

Dan, the promoter, kept sending up bouncers to warn us to turn down the volume but, in general, he was happy, and it was with great delight that I watched this smooth operator pay off two plainclothes detectives from the city's finest.

"What was that for, Dan?"

"That's to open the doors each night; that's the way it is," he answered, matter of factly. This man knew his way around the Apple's core. He had to, to stay in business, and I was mightily impressed by his operation. He knew how the city worked and used his talent to ensure that his little bits of the various boroughs ran with well-oiled wheels.

Playing in the ballrooms in Ireland in the 1960s, the audience was, naturally, all white. There may have been the odd black man or woman and an even odder Asian body, so it didn't strike me as a bit peculiar that the same colour pattern was replicated in the Irish clubs in the States. Nobody thought that, seeing as how we were in America's melting pot of worldwide immigration, it was a bit strange for the crowd to be all pale skins.

Billy and I saw an ad for Wilson Pickett, James Brown and The Chambers Brothers at the Cheetah. It was a Sunday afternoon show in the depths of Harlem and we made tracks to this soul festival. We ignored the taxi-driver's warnings about going into a dangerous place and when we alighted at the door of the famous club, we could hear the mad sounds from inside. The ticket seller took a long look at the two Irish exiles with the funny accents and had great difficulty understanding what we were trying to say.

"What time is Brown on at?" asked his namesake and I could see that this well-rounded woman was having major trouble making him out.

The bouncers weren't too sure about us either, but we didn't pay them too much attention. Inside, the heat was stifling and the joint was jumping. As it jumped, it was being passed from smoker to eager smoker, each set of lips sucking and inhaling the joy. The music was about twice as loud as our own band, and that was saying something in those days. The band onstage was the Chambers Brothers. There were no seats, just a couple of bars – one each side of the club – and a balcony that served its purpose in servicing the non-musical requirements of the patrons.

Four giant, slender black men, dressed in immaculate blue suits and ties, dominated the small stage. They had, at that moment, finished up a number and were politely accepting the applause when the only other white man in the Cheetah, their drummer, struck up a low, slow, barely audible rhythm. He played it while the four big men out front just stood motionless, staring out above our heads and looking like men who were receiving an important message from the gods.

The guitars and low-vamping harmonica entered the fray and started to play a riff over and over and over and over again. It was hypnotic. The place went into a trance and eyes were rolling in black faces as Brown and I looked on in amazement. On and on it went. They would lift the volume, ever so slightly, but the tempo never wavered. I began to get bored, hoping one of them would stand up to the mike and let fly, but the thing just kept repeating. Boredom vanished and was replaced by a primitive desire to move, to sway, to boogie. Turning to the Larne man, I could see that his head was sliding back and forth with this deranged repetition and on it still went. Holy Jaysus, start singing you fucker, was the thought in my brain. All I had was a couple of stiffeners before the taxi ride and my mind was starting to rebel but, just as quickly, I relented. I went with it and they kept playing, on and on and on. One of them moved up to stand before the same Shure mike we used ourselves, but it was a false dawn. The band kept weaving its spell. By now the thing was starting to hurt and I thought my head would burst wide open if one of them didn't kick it off, but it just stayed the same. This is what it must have been like when they were children in Mississippi, singing their gospel songs and trying to soul-heal their audience.

They had succeeded in turning the riff into the brightest gospel in Harlem, and the congregation, in a psychedelic trance, was receiving the word.

Then the highest voice I ever heard shouted from the Cheetah bandstand "The best things in life are free!" and the crowd went crazy. The spell was broken, and now it was safe to move your whole body in all kinds of whatever which way you chose. These boys really knew how to do it.

The Brothers brought the house down. They weren't making it easy for the rest to follow, but that is how it should be. These men had left the impoverished south, ventured to California and were now back east, trying to carry the message. I clapped my hands and roared at the top of my voice. They were magnificent.

"Look at the honky." She was laughing, pointing her long, slender, black finger into my face. She was beautiful.

I didn't know how to respond to the "honky" bit, but I was fairly certain about chatting her up.

"You're a right honky, yourself," was about the best I could muster over the noise of the band, who were still mesmerising the devotees, and she collapsed laughing.

She grabbed me around the waist and immediately began mickey-dancing, while at the same time endeavouring to explain that a honky couldn't call a black momma a honky. The serpent jumped to life in this heady mixture of excitement, gospel revival, and imminent joy. The Brown fella was engaged himself in another exploratory mission and deciding against the taxi-driver's advice was looking like the best call we'd made in New York.

"You can't call me that, honey," came dripping from her lips.

"You can call me anything you like as long as we sway like this," was my only reply.

And we just swayed the sinful sway, whilst the good gospel men from down south sang a gut-wrenching version of the Otis Redding hit "I've Got Dreams to Remember".

It was a beautiful situation to be in and I felt really at home, but the serpent was howling for action. As there was no wagon, hearse, or hotel room handy, I suggested the balcony and she said that the brothers used that area for entertainment of an entirely different kind.

"You stay outta there, honky; you get rolled."

If only, my poor head was thinking.

Meanwhile Billy had rejoined us and was discussing the Brothers' performance, when another round of screaming alerted us to Wilson Pickett striding onstage with a serious look in his eye.

"The Land of a Thousand Dances" man sang his big hit at twice the normal speed, making me think that he either wanted it out of the way real fast, or he was under the influence of something of a chemical nature that was telling him to "hurry up for fuck's sake".

His tongue was making the words faster than his demented voice could spit them out. Eyes standing out like Megahy's, he was a man in another dimension. He started belting it out, somewhere near the roof space, and just kept winding it higher and higher until I was sure the veins in his neck would burst.

I saw one of the fabulous soul brothers from

Mississippi standing watching all this and approached him. I invited him for a drink, which he graciously accepted, and we all trooped through the throng and fought our way to the most wired barman that ever served a drink in Harlem. There was no such thing as giving an order, you just took what he slapped on the counter in front of you and handed over the dollars. And it worked just fine. Sure why would a man be bothering another hard-working, spaced-out moonwalker by looking for a choice? If you wanted to get pissed, this is the stuff. Pay up and fuck off. And leave a tip, honky.

A lot of competing emotions were going on in my excited head. The racial abuser was hanging around my waist, and I was staring into the beautiful eyes of this big, gentle, psychedelic playboy from the Chambers Brothers. By now the serpent was panting to get near. Wilson Pickett was howling about his woman and the pain she was causing him and the temperature in the steamy, mirrored club was at boiling point.

The man was about six foot six in height and looked down on us all. We were joined by the white drummer and his was the only name I caught in the hubbub: it was Brian Keenan.

We drank and invited them all to the club we were playing in that night and said we could all have a real good Irish session after our dance. We warned them in advance that, even though we didn't do our original songs in the show, we had lots and maybe we could do something or other together later on.

The women, for Mr Brown had his own fan club, saw us to the door of the Cheetah and into the taxi and promises of new beginnings were made for later.

To miss James Brown was a tragedy but we'd our own show to get to.

"There's someone at the door looking for you, Derek, but I'm afraid they can't come in."

This was what the big door manager said just as we were about to go up for our first show of the evening. I had continued on drinking in the club after we had left the Harlem hotspot, and my head wasn't registering the problem. I knew the guys from the Cheetah were coming and had raved about them to a couple of the band and I imagined that they couldn't get in because they must have been in bad shape from the drink, or maybe something else they had been taking.

"They can't come in because they're black," was the bald, matter-of-fact statement he followed up with and I nearly died with shame.

I ran down to the front door and there was a mini verbal going on and it soon became apparent that, no matter what I said or threatened, they were not coming in. Brian Keenan wasn't with them, just two really fine, big, black, smiling gentlemen. Dan wasn't around but the bouncer assured me that, even if he had been, the result would still be the same. No blacks allowed.

All I could do was cringe and apologise to the Chambers Brothers and assure them that it wasn't like that in Ireland, or something equally pathetic. They just kept smiling and let me know that this was something they were used to; this was America. As a last resort, I threatened not to sing that night, but I was assured by this straight-talking New Yorker that the tour would be cancelled the following day. The rule would still be the same and nobody gave a shit anyway. Needless to say, the beautiful woman from earlier didn't appear either, or maybe she did and was met with the *céad míle failte*, New-York style.

So the wheel had turned full circle. Those whose ancestors had been forced to leave the "old country" because of hardship, intolerance, persecution and all the rest of it, had simply changed sides. They had forgotten. Instead of "No Catholics Need Apply", it was now "No Blacks Allowed In". And everybody, including the musicians, put up with it. Truth to tell, the next day it was all forgotten about.

Davy and I went to Tony Bennett's opening night in the Copacabana. He was sold out and the supporting comedian-singer was a real New-York riot. He had the crowd in tears of laughter, but my drummer pal and I couldn't understand a word he said. The joint, packed with the city's posh and bejewelled brigade, roared their approval at this man's every word. The ladies at the opening night were most unlike their Harlem sisters; these were horny women of the finest order and it was doubtful if the older, dotterin' daddies who seemed to be accompanying them would have had the ability to meet their demands. But, in those days, I didn't understand the true meaning of the pageant. The older and more senile the escort, and the more jewellery and fur wraps on show, the better you seemed to be doing. It was as if the biggest boast was, "Mine is older and richer than yours, bitch, so back off outta my face, I'm the Queen here."

As I say, I wasn't fully versed in the intricacies of the posh nightlife or diamond-driven society.

And opening night at the Copa was certainly an occasion to strut.

A twelve-piece band announced the star attraction with a pulsating riff, as the middle of the floor opened and up came the main man himself, singing out with his gifted voice; a true celebration of the art. With his unrivalled vocal control, Tony Bennett was note perfect, soul perfect, charm perfect. He pulled the place apart with his vocal gymnastics and when he sang "I Left My Heart in San Francisco", the women in the crowd went wild.

Bobby Hackett was playing in the band and Bennett made a big deal of featuring his mastery of the cornet in several solos during the show. He blew his thing with the controlled breath of a man who had mastered his art and who understood better than anyone else the exact amount of pressure needed to seduce the ear. He was renowned for his easy-listening style and was so smooth that listening to him merited the admission price on its own.

We made a beeline to the bandstand after the gig had finished and found him to be a most cordial fellow. He had never been to Ireland, but had heard great things about the country. He knew of only one Irish musician, he said, the great Gay McIntyre. Boy, did I feel good. You see these were the days before U2, when Ireland wasn't even a dot on the musical landscape. It hadn't happened yet.

Hackett had played with the best, including Glenn Miller, and it was he who blew the beautiful solo on the latter's big hit "String of Pearls", so it made me kind of proud that he knew about one of our own, the celebrated jazzman from Derry. I felt like telling this American legend that it wasn't a long way from Derry to Strabane, but desisted.

It was a hot place that night and it was even

hotter in a bar in downtown Manhattan a couple of days later when we went to see the king of drums, Gene Krupa. It was advertised in a local paper and we couldn't believe our eyes when we saw this drum legend playing his famous press rolls, and the rest, on a bar counter. There was some difference to the Bennett gig. Here was the man who, more than any other, had turned the art of drumming around. He'd made the drums practically a solo instrument. He was responsible for the advent of the tunable tom-tom and, for the love of God, had a movie made about his life, featuring Sal Mineo.

Playing on a fuckin' bar counter. It was a sight for saddened eyes. He played with all the skill that had made him a household name and smiled at one and all as he hit the skins and commanded them to dance like I'd never heard before. Like many a man before him, Gene had known the big time, jail time, small time, and now, rock-bottom time. Playing in a kip, trying to drink the shame away. He was in no mood to talk to a few Paddy groupies, and we left it at that. But he was immense, even then.

McKnight and I were trawling Times Square on the lookout for some action when we came across a club that simply declared: "Inside Cossack Nude Dancers".

That's all it said. It wasn't made clear if this was some kind of examination of the innards of a Russian dance troupe, or, with a bit of luck, a steamy sex orgy involving the famous horse people, but it stopped us in our tracks.

"Jaysus, Davy, we have it, we're on."

We approached this old lady who was at the door and asked about showtime and how much it was and the rest.

"Every half hour boys, come inside."

I thought it was a bit funny that we were the only punters in the place and, when we tried to enter the cordoned off area, we were told by the old dear that this was for VIPs when they ventured around.

Sitting down with a couple of expensive drinks, we waited ... and waited. Then, over the tannoy came a drum roll, music and flashing lights.

And on she came. The old dear, bollick-naked except for a tiny G-string, sporting leather boots up to her knees and wearing a Cossack hat. Ah, fuck me, we went hysterical. I nearly fell out of the chair and was holding onto the drummer man as we bayed with delight.

She was kind of hunkered over and attempting to kick the boots out in front of her, like a naked granny doing the Yenka. Keeping in perfect time with the music, her crossed arms were hiding the wrinkled, bouncing breasts and I, for one, was very happy about this. It was clear that on about every third or fourth bounce, her tiny backside made contact with the floor, but it made no difference. This lady was the real, original, super trooper. I thought my throat was going to constrict as rivers of salty tears ran down my cheeks and into my howling mouth. And she kept it up.

Never mind that two semi-hysterical men were collapsing in fits straight in front of her, she danced her little legs off. It seemed to go on forever but the wee woman didn't flinch. Then, when it finally ended, she stood up and made a most exaggerated bow, as if to say, well, at least you got your money's worth.

We stood and clapped her off and tried to shout for more, but it was impossible. We were still gaga with the laughter as we headed back into the night and Times "Unforgettable" Square.

The drive to Boston in the scorching sun on the Friday was in the tour manager's convertible Mustang. There were three wagons going to the gig – one for the gear and two for the band – and I drew the lucky straw and won my seat in the American sports classic. I rode the whole way with no shirt on and by the time we got to Massachusetts, my skin was lobster pink. Drinking beer and listening to the radio all the way up the highways, turnpikes, tolls, and freeways, I was absent from, what you might call, reality.

"I'm dyin' for a piece of black ass," the horny driver kept repeating. "Up here, they're everywhere, and outside the club they're on regular patrol."

These are the words he used. It sounded like there was an army of black women marching up and down and protecting the safety of the Irish clubbers, but I knew what he was on about.

"Are you up for it, Bigman?" and he was off again, talking to himself, sipping from a beer bottle and fantasising about his "black ass".

The gig was sheer agony. I was burnt to a cinder and, in an attempt to ease the pain, had rubbed calamine lotion into the skin, but it seemed to harden and made it worse, if anything, when I started jumping around the stage. I had a decent dose of liquor on board to help, but was relieved, nonetheless, when the gig ended. We were signing the photos and having the *craic*, when the black-assed driver came striding, purposefully, up to the stage.

"Derek, I want you for a minute."

I wasn't in any nick for bending or leaning forward, so I went over to the side of the stage to hear what he had to say.

"Man, I've got two of 'em outside. They can't come in, but will you come out and talk to them? C'mon."

I genuinely hadn't a clue what he was on about. At that precise moment, all I was interested in was getting back to the Big Apple and getting something done about the aching sunburn.

"Two what?"

"Black hookers, for fuck's sake. You said you wanted some."

I was mad keen of course, but it struck me immediately how he had turned this fantasy of his around and was now making me the main mover. But I was his man.

Outside, in the cool of a Boston summer evening, standing slightly to the left of the main ballroom entrance, I saw our two ladies of the night. One was Ella Fitzgerald and the other Diana Ross. It wasn't them, of course, they just looked like them and it was Ella who did the talking.

The big tour manager was swigging like crazy from a bottle of Jack Daniel's and I joined him as I listened to the fare.

"Seven dollahs a blowjob and ten a lay."

"A what? What's that again?"

For I had never heard such talk before. In those days, in Ireland, a blowjob was done in a hairdresser's and a lay was done either by a chicken or goose. In a riding man's lexicon in St Patrick's Island, the mighty deed was known by all sorts of names – I'll not bore you with them here – and the mouth-to-reptile resuscitation treat was known only, and ever, as "the gobble".

"Yuh know, seven a blow and ten a lay," she repeated.

At this stage the roadie was beside himself with horn and the girls briefly explained what they meant. But it was the first time I had ever heard this new lingo. To get laid and enjoy a blowjob is common parlance today, but that night in Boston I marvelled at their wonder.

"We take a taxi to our place and you guys follow behind."

Two of the brethren joined myself and the Mustang, black-ass man and we followed their ride to a built-up area about a couple of miles from the club. The rest of the lads remained behind, packing up the gear and urging us to be quick, as they needed a lead back to New York.

The six of us stood in a small room, which the girls used to complete the business before any action could happen, and it was Ella who collected the money. As soon as she had it in her possession, I saw that she moved to the window and drew the curtains across in an exaggerated fashion. Then she repeated the action and it appeared she was sending out some kind of signal. But we didn't care. Here we were in touching distance of adventure, and no man was calling halt.

Poor Ella was well used to rejection, for she took the news that we all wanted to spend our money on Diana without a flinch.

The room was divided by a string door of dangling beads and it was on the other side that the sinning took place.

The tour manager decided that he was on for a hairdresser's special, a fact that somewhat surprised me after all his talk.

He didn't keep us waiting for too long and I was up next, with the serpent leading the way, to partake in the more exciting chicken run. All sunburn was forgotten about and the Jack Daniel's tasted very sweet as we set about our business of love. That's exactly what it was – business – and something inside me kept telling my head that I didn't have enough drink on board to enjoy this. The whole affair was too clinical, and with a couple of giggling musicians peering through and shaking the beaded drop lines, the mood wasn't exactly made for romance. At least with the grandmother in London there was a bit of *craic* involved.

And the serpent caught the mood exactly. He bade a hasty farewell to this delightful, ebony-skinned lady of the night and I went back outside to drink some more with the now blubbering roadie. He was singing at the top of his voice and only stopped when he realised that in his pocket were the keys to the wagon that was carrying the gear. He insisted on leaving, but we were having none of it. We were all in this together; fuck him and the boys, they could wait.

We finally got back to the ballroom to find some pretty sore and peeved musicians. The wagon was packed, but they couldn't get into it and were wasting time waiting for the keys so they could get out of Boston and back to the Woodward. I vaguely remember Maurice shouting about how we were a pack of worthless fellows and the other lads being of roughly the same opinion. After they had gone, the roadie opened another bottle of booze and we sat smoking in the car and laughing about our encounter with the two black bombers.

The next thing I became aware of was coming to my senses out of a blackout and being stopped at traffic lights, with me behind the wheel of the Mustang. Its owner and one of the lads were sound asleep in the back seat, but we were in New York, the Bronx. One moment I was drinking in Boston and the next I was driving in New York. I looked at my watch and it was nearly six and tugged at the big Kerryman to wake up.

I had never before driven a left-hand drive car, especially down the turnpike from Massachusetts to the Big Apple, with its three or four toll booths and serial interruptions, but apparently I had just done that.

All I got from the Mustang's owner was a drunken grunt and a shuffle of position in the seat. I began to shout at him and he came to.

"Good man Derek, you did well," he said, or something similar, and he got out of the back and took over.

I couldn't believe that I had actually done it and we were all still alive. How do you drive over 200 miles and not know anything about it? And do it in a strange car, with all sorts of unaccustomed driving positions, like a left-hand gear lever, and not know a thing about the route? We were lucky men to be alive and when he was driving us to the Woodward and back to safety, I had another swig of the whiskey to settle down.

I don't remember leaving the Big Apple to come

back home. What is vividly clear is sitting on the plane at Shannon, trying to put on a shoe that seemed too small for my foot. I was trying to use my thumb as a shoe-horn and had torn its skin. I was pressing and pushing when the stewardess appeared.

"Sir, you'll have to leave the plane."

Peering out the window I saw the name, Shannon Airport.

"It's OK, I'm going to New York, and I'm trying to get this bloody shoe on."

"Sir, you're back from New York and you're the last person on board, so come on, you have to leave."

I had the parched mouth and enlarged licker once again, a state which I was becoming accustomed to as a regular outcome every time I drank. Journeys out were getting confused with journeys in, and they had a knack of merging at the point of utter befuddlement.

I found out in the lounge that, that same night, we were booked to play two venues in Cork City – the Arcadia and the City Hall. It wasn't a mistake; the Demp believed we could fill both of them.

And he was proved correct. It was a hell of a night, or should I say nights. It was some way to kick off again after the American hiatus, and we couldn't have restarted the eternal tour in a more exciting place. Feet wouldn't touch the ground and heads were heading right into and above the clouds, for a long time to come.

THIRTEEN

Papa oo

Peter Dempsey hadn't travelled with us on the American adventure. He was busy keeping the show on the road in Ireland and that was, of course, our priority. But I think that not going to the States was a bad move for the man. We began to imagine that we could do better. We should get a man from the South, a man who had more connections than our Belfast manager and who could give us a mightier push in our climb up the ladder.

We were in the top ten bands in the land by this stage, but it seemed that Dublin still wasn't happening. The Demp told us that there was a block on Northern outfits in the capital and there was nothing he could do about it.

In our lust for more, we fired the decent man. He was a big fan as well as being a great man for the *craic*, but we all gave him the big heave-ho. He didn't deserve it. What he said was being confirmed by other Northern band managers, but we didn't wish to hear. The band owed him for all his powerful work in establishing us as a major force on the scene, and we rewarded him with the sack. It was the first introduction of the "Jim Reeves syndrome", as it came to be known after his big hit "He'll have to Go". And when the sacking starts, it's hard to stop; but more of that later.

Our attitude was simple. If a man can't get you dates in the big Dublin venues, then get a man who can. And we got the best.

Oliver Barry was the greatest manager I ever worked under. He had a sharp brain and a head for facts and figures that was amazing. He knew the business inside out and had worked his way from Banteer in County Cork to the top of the tree in the showband industry, via the civil service and the Department of Agriculture.

His office was on Parnell Square just up from O'Connell Street and there was never a day that he didn't have something new happening. He was an exciting guy to be around and the proud owner of a wicked sense of humour. His office was a busy place as he looked after Sean Dunphy and the Hoedowners and a couple of other acts, including the Wolfe Tones.

And, being a non-drinker and having an abhorrence of cigarettes, he built his reputation as an all-action man.

"We must get a major hit and then record an LP lads," was his first suggestion. "And the more original stuff you do on it, the better."

He contacted Terry Wogan, who was making

waves with the BBC at the time, and organised a deal whereby we would record some jingles for his show. In those days, before you were allowed to broadcast to the UK, you had to pass a recording test, which was held in the Aeolian Hall on New Bond Street in London. This was done in Studio 2, which was to feature many of the great radio performances in the 1960s, from the Beatles to Bowie.

We were well received by the Beeb and the jingles for Wogan sounded good and won us a regular slot on his show, which had a huge and growing audience, and the good word about the Freshmen was beginning to spread around England.

Oliver used these appearances to connect with the big English record labels, but it was a hectic time in the music biz "over beyond" and there were hundreds of bands vying for any deal going. As we were making good money in Ireland, there was no desperation to sign, the way a lot of the English groups were forced to. After all, when the English bands had a decent chart success, the first thing they did was to organise a short tour on the showband circuit to make a few bob. There were no outlets in the British circuit like we had in Ireland. Either you were massive, like the Beatles or the Stones and played the really big venues, or you stayed at home.

It has been said many times that the big money was both a boon and a bogey for the big showbands. Why bother going through the pain required to promote a record in England, when there was serious money to be made on your own doorstep?

Irish groups, on the other hand, who had a very small and much less lucrative marketplace, were forced to emigrate to succeed, and they reaped their rewards by coming back home as conquering heroes. It was the same for them. No work in England, but if you could boast of a hit there, then bigger venues would open up in the land of saints and scholars.

We had been working on our harmony and trying to come up with something that could give us a real identity, and, bearing in mind that original songs are always the lifeblood of any musical style, we started writing in earnest for the planned album.

We travelled to Dublin for a couple of days' recording in our continuing quest for a hit single, and decided to do an arrangement of the old Chris Montez classic, "Let's Dance".

The slightly contradictory logic was that, until we proved capable of writing our own stuff, we should take a standard and make it so different that people would be seduced all over again by its charm, yet still appreciate the new arrangement. The Brown man took to the task with relish.

It was a terrific version of the old hit; full of running harmony lines that were arranged to rest over a slight change in the chord sequence from the original. But the best, and most difficult harmony, was held back until the fade-out.

Here it changed key and the voices rose in one pitch and came back down in a different one. It was very intricate, and if you ever get a chance to hear it, listen for this ending. We rehearsed it over and over, and when we got to the killing field, we could have sung it backwards.

The session was booked for just the two days and we devoted all our time to getting it just right. There was a fair bit of double tracking and we sang the blasted thing for all but a couple of hours of the session. But we were happy with the finished result. On a rough mix in the sound room, it came across as a winner. It was really fresh, if you pardon the pun, and all hands agreed the effort we put in was worth it and a big hit was on the way.

As we were standing around the engineer's chair, he asked, "What have you got for the B-side lads?"

In those vinyl days, a single had an A-side and a B-side. All very fair and balanced, but we hadn't given any thought to what was to go on the reverse.

"What about that thing we do, 'Papa oo Mow Mow?'" I ventured, thinking to myself that it would be interesting to hear how I sounded with the big gulderin' intro that the ditty featured.

"Get real for Christ's sake," was the outraged reply. "Cop on to yourself. Do you want to make us sound like a circus band?"

Not one of your better ideas, I thought to myself, while the brethren tossed their thoughts hither and thither.

As we were very short on time, there was a change of heart, and it was decided to put it down, as no one ever listened to B-sides anyway.

I think we had it done and dusted in about two hours, if it took that long. We just rattled it off and left the studio, myself included, in the belief that we had just recorded our first major hit. We were right, as it happened, but we were wrong at the same time.

Oliver rang me to say that our new record was being voted on in the most popular pop show of its day, BBC's *Juke Box Jury*. This was an American import with a British jury of pundits who voted the playlist a hit or miss by either smashing the vinyl or ringing a bell. It was a powerful show and had a major influence on what records made it to the charts. It was never really my cup of tea, as I always believed that, most of the time, they didn't know what they were talking about. I was with my girlfriend, Yvonne, in Dublin and the reception at the time for English stations was poor, to say the least.

Still, I settled down to watch it with a feeling of great excitement and apprehension. What if they voted it a miss? But at least we were on the programme. Not too many, if any, bands had made it to the *Jury*. This was just another example of Barry's clever promotion, his ability to get things done.

It leapt out of the TV set.

"A Papa oo Mow Mow, a Papa oo Mow Mow."

They were playing the wrong track.

The camera tracked the faces of the guests and commentators and the show's presenter, David Jacobs, was tapping his fingers and smiling broadly. Jaysus, it was sounding great. They stopped halfway through and all heads nodded in agreement. This was going to be a smash. They loved it and predicted it would race to the number-one spot and give this Irish band, The Freshmen, their big break into England. I danced around the small room, hugging my equally excited lover and swore that this particular set of judges were the most knowledgeable ever assembled. Good old "Papa oo".

The carousel began to spin at ever-increasing speed. Promoters all over the country wanted to host the band in venues, some of which I'd never heard of before. Huge sums were offered and we hurtled into a whirlwind of gigging, recording, drinking, sexing, earning, and I believed that, no matter what happened, this would never end.

The disc sold well and was never off the radio in Ireland. We had several records released since "The Yenka", including a dastardly follow-up, "King Cole Yenka", best left unremembered, but by and large it was true to say that we hadn't set the radio stations many selection problems in determining their playlists. Most of our stuff had to be promoted heavily with the odd dropsy to radio producers and deejays, but with "Papa oo" the trouble was in keeping up with it.

The charts at that time were, I suppose, as accurate as they are today. It is impossible to track, efficiently, the sales of records with any degree of scientific accuracy. Best-sellers lists are, at best, a snapshot of a nation's preferences, and these indicators are determined by checking with a selected number of record shops.

The figures are, and were, open to manipulation in all the many ways a manager, band, promoter or publicist could imagine. Of course, business insiders know all the relevant outlets and this leads to the non-startling attempts to buy the hits.

So it was as natural as ninepence that the showband heads stroked like mad with the chart standings. And it was a given too, as I said, that a good manager could use his contacts to ensure that whatever record you had out was played on the radio and the word was spread that the bloody thing was selling like wildfire. Every record was a hit in the showband days. There were no misses. It was the same for everyone.

But now and then there were genuine hits. Songs that people just went crazy over and we were just plain lucky that "Papa oo" was one of them. These records would be played on every show, and one of the real tests of a genuine smash was if you heard back that the other bands were doing it in their programme. And they were.

Young mothers would approach you at dances and tell you how their infants would start to jump about and shake their cradles when it came over the radio. It had no introduction, like most pop songs, and the strange bass voice at the beginning was an immediate attack on your eardrums. This made it handy for radio presenters to open a show, or use it as a pick-up after a set of ads or chat. It was guaranteed to get your attention.

It joined the ranks of the showband hits of the 1960s and stands beside other mega mind-blowers such as "The Hucklebuck" from Brendan, "Old Man Trouble" from Doc, "Candy Store on the Corner", Dickie's crowd-pleaser, and others like, "Make Me an Island" from Joe Dolan and, of course, Eileen Reid's unforgettable lament, "I Gave My Wedding Dress Away".

Oliver was now in the position to pick and choose and had organised a short trip to London, like the Demp before him, so that some major players over there could see and hear us perform. He had arranged a meeting with Colin Berlin, a major promoter who worked closely with artists such as Tom Jones, Englebert Humperdinck and, as we were soon to discover, had a promotional contract or something with The Who. He was a big-time boy who controlled a major slice of what was going down in the world capital of the industry – London.

Billy and I were invited to the meeting with

Oliver and the cigar-smoking bigwig of pop, and all hands arrived at Berlin's office at ten o'clock on a Monday morning. We had a gig that night in the Hammersmith Palais, but that was of minor importance compared with meeting this guru of dreams, and was well to the back of our minds.

We waited in the reception area, covered in big framed photos of all his acts, and a man couldn't have been anything other than impressed by the aura of success surrounding the place. There were a lot of famous faces looking down from the walls of the reception area.

There were no losers in this lot; there was no failure here. This was going to be another leap into the unknown fantasy world of, well, fantasy. I just wanted more. Of what, I wasn't sure, but it was along the lines of what we already had at home. Fame, money, sex, adoration, fame, sex and celebrity. Oh, and plenty of the rest of course. More fame, drink, food, more drink and a little more fame, please. That would have been a fair enough reflection of what was going through my big excited head that morning as I sat beside Barry and Brown waiting to be taken into the Temple of Dreams, the place where no man would leave disappointed after having charted a course through the clouds and right up into the Pearly Gates of Your Own Backside and more fame.

Mr Berlin, the archetypal Jewish promoter, had a bald head and smoked a big long Cuban cigar. He was a most welcoming host and greeted us like long-lost rich cousins who hadn't made a will. He said that he understood there was a lot of hot stuff coming out of Ireland and he knew we were to the forefront of the gold rush.

"Call the Beeb and find out what number 'Papa oo Mow Mow' is this week," he commanded his beautiful secretary. Her mini-skirt had caught the serpent's attention during our wait for admission to this inner sanctum, but I reprimanded him and thought that this was a time to focus on more important matters.

"Number 50," was the telephoned reply.

We were all high as kites, well at least Brother Brown and myself were; Oliver had a calmer head for business.

Mr Berlin puffed on his cigar and was in the middle of outlining our approach to international stardom when the door opened and in walked two members of The Who – Keith Moon and Pete Townsend.

It was obvious these men didn't wait in reception rooms, for the big cigar man warmly greeted them before suggesting that we should all meet up later. It was heady stuff being introduced to these superstars as fellow travellers, and we struck up a brief conversation whereupon the two lads invited us to join them after the meeting in a club they frequented nearby. It was agreed we would follow on and further cement Anglo-Irish rock relations.

Berlin announced how he would organise a quick-fire tour to Australia and New Zealand that would take in a couple of gigs, but which would be primarily concerned with promoting the record. He was amazed when we told him that our show lasted two hours and recommended that, henceforth, thirty minutes with a couple of "tabs" or encores, would be our lot. He and Oliver discussed the business

end of it all, but our heads were away in Bondi
Beach, celebrating freedom with lines of bikini-clad
nymphettes. I could smell sweet scents on sweaty
bodies and was mentally practising a judicious bit
of boomerang-throwing.

We arranged to meet again later on that evening
for a meal in a posh Covent Garden restaurant, and
Bill and I scurried off for our rendezvous with The
Who. Boy, this was really living.

"You take these little yellow boys first thing in
the morning, and then, about halfway through the
day, you take one pink. If you are drinking, you stay
away from the white ones, but if you're not, then it's
OK to have a couple before you play," prescribed
Keith Moon as we sat in a quiet corner of a private
members' club frequented by Berlin. His eyes were
dancing underneath a shock of hair which had a
rainbowish colour, as he laid out in front of him on
the table an array of tablets with enough combined
power to sink a battleship. He was emphasising
that this was a much better way to go than the triple
whiskeys Bill and I were downing. But through all
this mad chemical advice, I could see that he was a
very shy man, totally at odds with the reputation he
carried with him.

Townsend wasn't into the "leapers", as Moon's
little helpers were known. He had done enough
speed to last a lifetime and was now in the process
of writing an opera. He was commenting about how
strange it was for a West Coast sound to be coming
out of Ireland, but we assured him that we were a
much-maligned nation in the UK press and, in fact,
you couldn't move in the west of Ireland without
bumping into super-cool, semi-stoned surfers and

their boards, all the way from Ballyshannon to Dingle. The ultra laid-back, guitar-wrecking genius knew it was a wind-up, but we laughed and drank some more.

The two Who soon departed, but Billy and I stayed on in the little club, sinking triple-whiskey shots and dreaming dreams. We were going to be doing an all-original set with no more covers. There was no sign of a "I've had enough switch" anywhere that afternoon, but the tempo was slowing down a bit as five o'clock approached and we remembered our dinner date with Oliver and the Guru. We steadied ourselves with a couple more drinks and arrived at the posh nosher, near enough on time.

The commissionaire on the door wasn't too sure about us in our slightly drunken state, but we managed to find the two impresarios and they secured our admission.

It was the biggest menu card I ever held in my hand. It was a huge thing with only about half a dozen main courses and when my eye lit on steak tartare, I was a happy man. There was very little steak tartare in Ireland, and certainly it was a rare thing indeed in the chippers around Belfast and Strabane, so a lad could be forgiven for his ignorance of the recipe. Finely chopped raw beef, along with peppers, capers, onions and various mustards was an unknown delight to my peasant's palate.

"I'll have the steak please, and make sure it's well done," I said, to a pause from the embarrassed waiter.

"Ahem, it's raw steak, sir."

"Well, cook the fucker, for Jaysus sake," was my uncouth reply and, to mutterings of disapproval of this oafish behaviour, I ordered the only other thing I could make out on the menu; roast hare.

I don't think that the Berlin-Barry axis was overly impressed with either of these two semi-demented, not-so-fresh men, but it was the 1960s, fuck it, and this was mild enough stuff.

I was standing holding onto the rail of the upper level balcony in the packed Hammersmith Palais, looking down at the couple of thousand or so people who were out for the night's *craic* in the giant ballroom. My oul head was swimming out against the tide and finding it a choppy night indeed. Somewhere in the back of my mind was a meeting with very famous men, sometime in the recent past, and also a drinking encounter with one of my idols, Brendan Bowyer. I wasn't too clear about any of this, and when I looked behind me and saw Brother Brown, stretched out and sound asleep on the big red sofa, it didn't help my cause.

Peering down again into the heaving crowd, I saw the strangest of things. There was a band playing on a stage directly in front of the crowd and, as the scene slowly unfolded to me, I made out the sound of the compère doing his usual end-of-show routine, "Thank you for being such a wonderful audience, and now I'd like to welcome from Ireland our star attraction tonight, the fabulous Freshmen."

On a stage, directly behind him and out of sight of the by-now excited exiles, I could see five lonely Freshmen starting to play our opening song as the stage revolved the 180 degrees. Holy Jaysus, I panicked. It's the lads, we're on; oh shit, and I shouted in Billy's ear as I grabbed him by the back of his collar.

"For fuck's sake, wake up Bill, let's go," and we hurtled down the steel spiral staircase and bounced our way out onto the ballroom floor.

I half carried, and half pushed, Ireland's greatest talent through the confused revellers. Reaching the front of the stage, which was too high for me to push us both onto, I enlisted the help of some bemused, and other highly amused, patrons. And fair play to the guys making the music, they didn't attempt to prevent this unruly invasion of their working space. They knew that there would be no contributions from this pair of legless wonderboys, but they stoically played on in the best tradition of the game.

Brown straightened himself up and, summing up all the power left in his fragile frame, he performed a sort of semi-conscious stagger across the stage and collapsed on top of his keyboard. It wasn't switched on, so there was no sound as he continued his slumber, so violently interrupted, a few minutes before.

The crowd was now going hysterical with laughter. They couldn't believe it and, deep down, I think they were secretly delighted. Sure they were probably all half-pissed themselves and seeing two warriors showing up unfit for duty brought out the best in them.

But although the abandoned musicians didn't prevent our boarding of the good ship Freshmen, the judgments from the bandstand were clear. There would be hell to pay later.

I waddled over to Damien, who was doing his best to batter out our opening number, and slabbered a drunken whisper in his ear, to the effect that better times lay ahead. Naturally, the poor man did his best

to ignore me and prodded me away with the neck
of his Fender.

I turned and shouted over the backing to the rest
that we were all headed for Australia; we were going
to be instant millionaires; we were going to play in
an opera, and anything else my shorting brain could
come up with. The situation was desperate. I had
visions of an attack of the "Jim Reeves syndrome"
coming on after the dance. I had to repair a bad
situation.

As soon as Damien stopped singing, the packed
house clapped their delight and I grabbed the mike
off its stand.

"Brendan Bowyer is in the hall and is going to
sing 'The Hucklebuck'," I roared.

"Put your hands together for Brendan, Ireland's
superstar. C'mon Brendan, get down here Brendan,"
and so forth. I needed some help and who better
to give it than the Showband king. If ever a man
guldered for aid, I did so that night.

The brethren had no other option than let me
continue this drunken rant until the great man
appeared and, beaming his wonderful shy smile,
took the spotlight. Needless to say, he pulled the
place apart.

The following week, "Papa oo" headed south in
the English charts, never to return, and there was no
more talk of Australia or, indeed, any further contact
with Mr Berlin. Our international breakthrough
would have to be put on the back burner, so it was
on with the merry-go-round back home. *Sic transit
gloria Bondi* (thus passes the glory of Bondi Beach).

FOURTEEN

The Shakes

We booked the Eamon Andrews studio in Dublin again and recorded our first album, appropriately entitled *Movin' On*. We put a mighty effort into it and featured original songs from several of the band. Most had a style which was dictated by Billy and it consisted of a prominent harmony build, up-tempo lead into a slower break, and a change of mood. It was like making love to a hungry woman and, just when the thing is getting ready to hit the ceiling, stopping and starting to play again, as if you were just beginning. The songs built up, and then changed direction, played around with vocal subtleties, before taking off again to a dramatic climax. It was an attempt to build a set of harmonic interludes, which, in their own right, would provide the "hook". We spent a lot of time rehearsing the flow of the songs and, I think, it was the best ever example of the band as a harmony unit. It was also the last time that the band would try and impress with our brass line on disc.

The work was recorded on a four-track machine and the engineer proved to be a bit of a star with the sounds he was able to extract from this fairly primitive set-up. He was a wizard, and proved again that what comes out of a recording machine is normally better than what goes into it. These guys were stars in their own right and, to my mind, were all worthy of the name Merlin.

I came to rely heavily on them, as I shall now describe.

The first time I ever sang in a recording studio was in London, during the "I Stand Alone" session. The band had played the backing track and, apart from finding it a bit unusual to go out into the room on my own and sing, I was cock-a-hoop and ready to proclaim myself as the next Elvis, Frank, Dino, Chuck, Johnny or Joe, or maybe a mixture of the lot of them. I wasn't a bit nervous and sang her with all my heart.

"Come in for a listen then, Derek," called Harold Geller, our producer.

I listened in shock horror. Oh my God, I thought. This can't be me. That whiney, creaky, wonky, wanky, pathetic voice isn't mine. There must be a mistake. He must have pressed the wrong fucking button or something. But it was me alright. He hadn't dressed it up, or added any special effects, but I still didn't like it when he did. The sound of my illusions shattering rang out all over the studio, and, try as I might that night, I couldn't change the one, overriding reality; I didn't like the sound of my own voice. You might say that it was an opinion shared by many, up and down the land.

But back to *Movin' On*. It was produced by the talented Mr Bill Sommerville-Large, who later went on to greater things in the music and film world. He and Billy struck up a good relationship, based, it was clear to see, on mutual respect.

We hyped the thing like mad, but though it included, "Papa oo" and won many admirers, it didn't produce another magic hit, but it stood the test of time and carried us along for the next couple of years. And exciting years they were.

At this time in the 1960s, Scott McKenzie's "San Francisco (Be Sure to Wear Flowers in your Hair)" was warning all and sundry that there was going to be a terrific love-in there and anybody with any sense was heading out west in the new love rush. The mind doctors, the hugely rewarded psychiatrists, who followed this goldmine of innocents in search of new clients, weren't yet in the business of dispensing their pharmaceuticals to help "balance" these flower-party animals. The flower-power sellers in concert fields, throughout this vibrant and awakening landscape, were distributing all the expensive drugs themselves. We looked across the Atlantic in awe as our American leaders spoke of the new dispensation of free love, the blossom bonanza – peace man, not war – and made beautiful music, all at the same time. What a winning combo.

People were experimenting with altered states of the mind and new gurus arrived on the scene to preach and spread the gospel of love. Every town in Ireland vied with the Golden Gate city to host the love-fest, and in ballrooms all over the land, singers,

The Theatre of the A**e on wheels!
(Courtesy of Sean Mahon)

At one time, we devised a new technique for fishing.
(Courtesy of Liam Glass)

This was our welcoming pose for the taxman.
(Photograph by Noel Doyle)

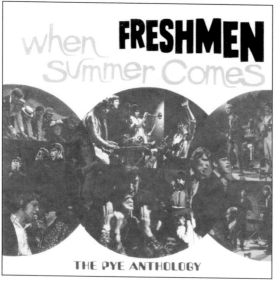

This is the original
album cover of
'Movin' On'.

Suffer the little minstrels to come unto me – the incomparable Billy Brown.
(Courtesy of Sean Mahon)

by KEN STEWART

Dance to 'The Yenka' is the freshmen's request

'La Yenka' took the country by storm.

Everybody's doin' it!

THE Yenka, announced in CityBeat last week, will undoubtedly reach 'craze' proportions within the next few weeks if the current trend is continued.

To-morrow the FRESHMEN have their record version released, and the band will be featuring it prominently at all future dates. Since they introduced it into their act a fortnight ago, there has not been a single dance that it has not been requested less than five times. And it's not only the Freshmen who are featuring it. The Victors from Cork have climbed on the bandwagon, and may have their version released soon. Other southern showbands including the Miami have taken it up—much to the delight of the Freshies.

'Every time another band plays it, it's a great plug for our record', says Derek Dean, who takes the floor to demonstrate at dance-dates. Here Derek outlines the basic steps. Dancers can improvise their own versions. So here goes!

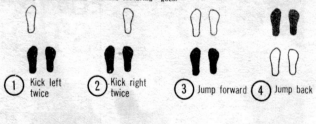

1. Kick left twice
2. Kick right twice
3. Jump forward
4. Jump back
5. Jump sideways to right 3 times. Repeat.

SIMPLE ISN'T IT? All your partner has to do is to stand opposite and kick right when you kick left, etc.

© Copyright Morton Newspapers Ltd.

A whole lot of kickin' goin' on.

We 'blattered' it to death – 'La Yenka', again!

Posing outside Queen's University Belfast.

Sixties 'rebel' casual gear.

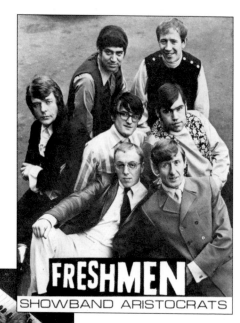

FRESHMEN
SHOWBAND ARISTOCRATS

Bill shows frustration… and in a calmer mood below.
(Courtesy of the *Sunday World*)

(Courtesy of the *Sunday World*)

New blood again: *(left to right)* John L Sullivan, Tiger Taylor, my good self and
Billy, with Trevor Boyce and Paddy Freeney at the front.
(Courtesy of the *Sunday World*)

Shine on Fat man – new addition Pat Carey *(bottom right)*.
(Courtesy of the *Sunday World*)

Micheál MacLiammóir looks on in awe as Bill tells him about
General Custer.
(Courtesy of Eddie Kelly)

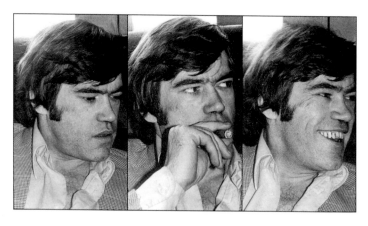

Innocence gone.
(Courtesy of the *Sunday World*)

including myself, were encouraging the wearing of hair flowers and as little else as possible. On a passing note, Scott didn't write this mega anthem of the day and broke his heart and head for years trying to get his hands on a follow-up. This world seller was recorded using a studio band, and piano on the session was played by a young Larry "three-hands" Knechtel, who featured more prominently in the beautiful Simon and Garfunkel classic "Bridge over Troubled Water".

The Beatles were encouraging the love-in with "All you need is Love", so there was this air of "love is the new drug", and it was gaining more and more addicts as the decade grew old. We all subscribed to the love therapy revolution: "if it was broke, Cupid's arrow would fix it."

It was the in thing to profess this new dogma, this cool theology of the hip. We didn't need governments or greedy politicians to steer the planet to survival; it would be done with a good mix of blow, speed, beer, melody, sex and liberation. This was all the healing you would ever need.

In fact, this was just a follow-on to the group therapy session I had witnessed one night as I watched Tom Dunphy of the Royal singing "Nobody's Child" at a show in Drogheda. And when I saw it for myself, its significance dawned on me. Nightly, we were polluted with requests to do this melancholic dirge, but nobody in the band would sing it. It was considered too "black puddin'" and best avoided. We were heading back North after a cancelled gig, and dropped into the Abbey cinema-cum-ballroom to see Brendan, Dunphy and the lads.

Rows and rows of mini-skirted young women

stood singing the lament, most with tears running down their cheeks. They sang in perfect pitch with the late bassman, as he professionally delivered the sadness and unfairness of it all. A poor, blind orphan's plight struck a major chord somewhere deep within their collective soul, and they were intent on getting it out. This poor unloved and unwanted child was an assault on their sense of justice and love. Let us hear all about it again, Tom, sing again about the poor little fucker, unseeing, abandoned and unwanted. It was a mass exorcism of self-pity, a soul-cleansing act that worked so well it had to be done again. We know the love is coming, Tom, and we don't want to spoil it with all this negative stuff; we have it deep inside, so come on man, get out the magic wand and play it again. He would have been singing it all night if the band hadn't called another tune.

That was the lot of the minstrel in the love generation. If a problem arose, then music and love would fix it. And this was the mindset of a young, mid-twenties Strabane rocker who deep down knew it wasn't so, but whose spirit was caught up in the never-ending carnival.

It was around this time that I married my girlfriend Yvonne. She was a slim, lissome head-turner from Waterford and we met in Dublin, where she worked as a part-time model and full-time office manager for *Spotlight* magazine. It was love at first sight for me and it took a fair bit of persuading for her to throw her lot in with a travelling bandsman.

I loved her sense of style; she was a natural. She had the kind of body that most women have to constantly diet for. Consequently, everything she wore looked great and, when we socialised, you could see a lot of hungry men with sinful stares.

She wasn't impressed by the fact that I sang with a top outfit. After all, her job brought her into contact with all the big names of the day, all the time, so it's fair to say, that she didn't impress easily. Still, we managed to make the connection and on the morning we wed, it was with a mad, crazy expectancy. She was doing the expecting, while I was supplying the mad and crazy.

I drank with a ferocious madness on the day of our wedding. It was as if I was telling myself that this was such a special day that the buzz had to be extra special as well. It was the usual Irish booze extravaganza, with me leading the way. I think that she enjoyed the early part, but she couldn't have been too happy when I stood at the top of an escalator in Heathrow Airport, later that night, and plummeted, head first, to the bottom, taking with me a couple of innocent fellow-travellers. It was a crazy honeymoon night, as the only memory I ever had of that first married evening was of coming out of a blackout with a pint of milk in my hand, standing outside our bedroom door. I had been to the reception area on this errand for my thirsty bride, in my underpants.

I was nearly the last of the Freshmen to marry and when we returned from our honeymoon, it was full steam ahead once again.

Married life suited us both. My new bride would travel to gigs when she fancied and there was a carefree vibe about the whole union. It felt good, and although I was drinking heavily, I just imagined that this was the way of all young married couples. We partied hard on nights off and when our first child was born, after a couple of years of relative harmony,

I felt I was a blessed man. Sinead Martina was a healthy little angel, and a couple of years after that again we were joined by Sorca Martina, another little winged wonder from Heaven. Life was wonderful and we had many a good night's *craic* in our Terenure home. Had we a son, it's a fair bet we would have called him Martin.

When the kids were a couple of years old, she began to mention my drinking and that it might be a good idea to cut back as it was affecting our lives and affecting us, not for the better. One unforgettable nightmare of a day brought this undeniable fact right into our living room.

We had been out the night before, in some pub or other, and when I approached the bar I ordered double vodka.

"Anything with it, sir?"

"Yes, a double brandy."

When the barman put the two drinks on the counter, I reproached him, "No, you don't understand. A double brandy with the double vodka. Put it in the vod."

This was the showbiz instinct, the show-off egomaniac, call it what you will, but the man behind the counter was amazed.

"Jaysus, I've never heard of that before," he said, looking to see what I would get for Yvonne.

"And a vodka and tonic for the lady."

I mixed the two drinks into a tumbler and milled it straight down the hatch. It burned and scorched my vocal chords on the way down, but I had to say it wasn't all that bad.

So, it was the same again, and again and again. I don't know how many Sillyman Hand Grenades

I took that night, or what I had to drink when I got back home, but the next day, I awoke with a feeling of splendid calm. It was a feeling of peace, which to this day has only ever been matched on one other occasion.

It was my usual wake-up time of about 2 p.m. and Yvonne, who had been up and about as usual with her work, came into our bedroom and asked if I would like a cup of tea brought upstairs.

This was the feeling the Gurus of Enlightenment speak of. I felt I could float downstairs and slide like a whisper into the big leather armchair, and politely refused her kind offer of a civilised start to the day.

I thought to myself that I had finally cracked it. At last, I know what to drink and not experience the dreadful hangovers that used to plague my soul. There was no guilt, no remorse, no desire for another, no restlessness, no head panic that it was all going to end soon and I would be the first to get it, or any other, similar shit, that I had become so accustomed to. Double vodkas with double brandy chasers. A bit expensive, but worth every penny for this bliss.

I floated into the big chair and waited for my afternoon cuppa. The kids were at school and things were tranquil in the Dean household, and my spirit was a well of healing balm.

Then, without prompting, the index finger of my right hand jumped up into the air and back down onto the leather armrest. As I turned my attention, about to chastise it for breaking the serene mood, it did exactly the same, except this time, it was accompanied by the middle finger. The two together and then it was the whole hand. It was shaking out of my control.

At once, my whole right hand side began to vibrate violently and I shouted for my wife. I was in a state of panic at this stage and believed I was experiencing a heart attack. By now, my whole body was jumping out of the chair and as it lifted off, it shot back again with neck-breaking speed. My teeth were chattering like a tap dancer on his board, whereupon a startled Yvonne ran screaming to the phone. She rang for assistance and then raced to a neighbour's for help. I suppose she panicked a bit too.

I felt my heart pound against my chest and believed for sure that it must break through. I have seen movies of electric shock being passed through a condemned man in the death chair, and that is how my body was rattling. It began to emit a low hum from somewhere deep down below and I pissed myself. I couldn't stop.

This was some way to go, was the thought which predominated my mind and I was wishing that it would hurry up and end this torture. I had absolutely no idea of how to stop the hurricane, and when my terrified wife and friend came running into the room her companion shouted and ran back to her own house. She returned with a naggin of whiskey and forced it into my mouth.

My teeth chipped the glass off the top of the little bottle as she pushed it in further so as it could get down my neck. I couldn't feel them, but I knew there were glass fragments on my tongue and I was coughing and sputtering as the brown liquid fought its way into my system. My throat was spitting it out, but my belly was sucking it in and, all the while, I was rocking the chair off its support. There was no stopping this damn curse; I was on the way out for sure.

The first thing to stop shaking was my tongue. I remember that clearly because, suddenly, it was able to trace the tiny pieces of glass lining the bottom of my gums. It didn't seem like a relief at first, but within a few moments the continuous eruption began to subside. The rattle of my teeth was causing me to bite the serpent's assistant, but I couldn't protect it.

After what seemed a lifetime of this brutal reverberation, it passed. There was no calm, but a state of extreme fear along with a deep embarrassment over having wet myself. My heart was still pounding and the only thing I knew for sure was more whiskey was required. I also had a complete understanding of the phrase used by the drinking classes to describe a hangover victim: "he looked a bit shook". Jaysus, I was in no doubt.

The doctor took one look at my big rattled head sitting lost on the chair and asked if I drank much.

"Oh, about a couple of pints a day," I lied, as drinking men often do.

The good doc was strangely sympathetic to a booze demon like myself. He turned to Yvonne and addressed her thus: "Don't be giving out to him and make sure he gets plenty of rest." It was a strange thing to say to an innocent bystander, but he probably wasn't up to bollicking his own missus, so another man's would do.

Turning back to me, the kind-hearted doc continued, "And limit your intake to a couple of pints a day. In the meantime, I'm gonna give you these tablets and you're to take three a day. They'll get you right as rain."

He called them Valium and it was the first I'd

heard of the tranquiliser that, along with the other little pill, would find its way into the purses of so many of our womenfolk.

Yvonne had brought back a bottle of whiskey as well as the tablets from the chemist and by now the shaking was completely gone. The little bit of juice had stilled the storm and I wanted to get some more on board before the lads came to the house for a six o'clock call.

It was about five o'clock and I worked it out with my relieved wife that as I hadn't taken one in the morning, and wouldn't bother taking them to Galway, I'd be better taking the three of them now and then start the one-tab-at-a-time routine the following day. There was no thought of Keith Moon as I swallowed them with a glass of whiskey and continued to sup until the departure time. But I had resolved to hit the vodka and brandy specials on the head. I ignored the little doctor's advice, of course, as most drinkers do and, besides, the last person you reveal the truth to is someone who is trying to help. At least, that's the way it was.

By the time the lads arrived, I was moonwalking around the lounge of my home. I couldn't feel my size thirteens as they groped for the red carpet and tried in vain to answer the door when they arrived. They left without me.

But I have jumped too far forward in this tale. While my wife and I were going from one drinking crisis to another, my whole hectic life as a road musician in a travelling, mainstream band, roared on.

Movin' On was released on the Pye Label and we plugged it as best we could. It was a stepping stone and we received great reviews, but there was a feeling abroad that it wasn't different enough to cut the mustard internationally.

The vinyl was still spinning on the turntables when Oliver announced that he had got us a deal with CBS.

This was big news as it was our first, and only, contract with a company based in London. The company was CBS UK as they had no office in Ireland at the time, and the talk was of us recording with top engineers and producers and coming up with an album that would succeed where our previous offerings had failed. If it was a hit in Ireland, then so much the better, but sales there didn't amount to much. Oh no, they insisted, we would be aimed at the international marketplace. Sure you couldn't beat it with a big stick.

One of the best studios in London at New Bond Street was booked, and the top producer of the day, Mike Smith, was assigned to the band. We were given a selection of songs to rehearse and arrange and, Don Gold, a dynamic young orchestral arranger, was contracted to write the arrangements for the ensemble, which was to be our backing. That band included some of the finest studio players in England and many had featured on major hits throughout the decade. Obviously CBS believed that only the best would do and they didn't rate our ability as tunesmiths. The Freshmen weren't to write the songs or play on the recordings; we were just to do what we were told. We went along, for who could have refused such an opportunity.

The new album also introduced a major shift in the workings and culture of the group. We had, by undertaking this venture and its approach to recording, unofficially designated ourselves as a vocal-harmony unit. It was a subtle shift that no one commented upon at the time, but it was to herald a dark future for Maurice, and in turn, the entire band.

Peace on Earth was the result of all this collaboration of talent, not actual peace of course, but that was the theme and lean of the work. It was a mould-breaker of sorts, as we became the first Irish band to record a "message" album and also because it featured the wonderful voice of a superstar, from another discipline, the mind-blowing Mícheál Mac Liammóir.

Barry had the vision to bring it all to life. Mac Liammóir was his suggestion, truth to tell, although I now describe the venerable actor as "legendary", in those days I'd never heard of him.

Billy spent great energy working on the, mainly mediocre, songs that we received on a tape from London. He listened, embellished, interpreted as best he could within defined limits, and arranged them, for and between us.

Oliver, Bill and I met Mac Liammóir in the old Hibernian Hotel on Dublin's Dawson Street for a most enjoyable lunch, at which it became apparent to me that this guy was bigger than the Freshmen would ever be.

His voice resonated all over the sedate dining room as he regaled us with tales of his thespian adventures. He was really enthusiastic about the project, whereby his voice would narrate the spoken links that would hold the theme together. He fell in love with Billy right there and then and was captivated by the Larne man's flowing, blond mane. But the sax man, not to be left behind in the entertainment stakes, was up for the occasion. As the celebrated actor marvelled at his flowing tresses and made to run his fingers through them, the bould Bill began.

"I'm a big fan of General Custer's, who wore his hair long as a taunt to the Apache nation," intoned Bill to the bedazzled actor/writer/director and bon vivant. There followed an afternoon of side-splitting stories narrated by one of the most compelling speaking voices I have ever heard. We parted as lifelong friends, or at least we said so.

Mícheál was gagging for it and wanted to get his voice lines as soon as possible, in order to start straight away on this "wonderful work". That's how he described it in a press interview on the release of the album.

It took many trips to England's capital to complete it. We never got to meet the Irish legend during the actual recording, as he had done his bit before we'd even started. But the producer assured us that he was a dream to work with, and was most patient and understanding at all the delays and retakes that were involved.

And that was the truth of it, as we would come to experience ourselves when it came to doing our bit. We had engaged with an obsessive producer, with a secret third ear, which insisted that everything could be better. His track record was impressive, having had a long list of hits, so there was no arguing with his ability, but he searched for a sound that was known only to himself.

He was recording five voices and he went to

great pains to settle the war in his head. Lead vocals
weren't too bad, but when it came to block harmony,
he demanded more. Even with the part of a song that
wasn't in harmony, multi-voice recording was a trial.
Nowadays it is commonplace for record producers
and engineers to spend days just mikeing drums
for a particular sound, but in New Bond Street in
the 1960s, it was unusual. We went to great lengths,
normally, to ensure that the offering would be the
best possible standard we were capable of producing,
but this man was pernickety beyond belief.

A couple of tracks in the collection are memorable,
namely "Banquet for the World" and "When God
Created Woman". The rest, I believe, are a mixture
of the instantly forgettable and the mediocre. The
idea was good, the theme excellent, the arrangements
exceptional, but the songs let it all down. It was the
first and last time we had bowed to the dictates of a
record company. We should have insisted on writing
them ourselves, but we had bought the dream and
sold the integrity.

"Banquet" featured Billy at his brilliant best; the
harmony lines are hypnotic and the band, behind
it all, outstanding. We released this as a single
sometime later, and it was a middling success but it
seemed to me that it didn't reach anywhere near its
full potential.

"When God Created Woman" is the only song
from that album that we used to feature regularly in
our stage show. It is a big ballad with choral harmony
and it used to go down very well. However amazing
it may seem to the reader, the truth is that Billy never
learned its words. He always had to sing them off
a sheet.

The production of one of the songs nearly drove me insane, even if there wasn't far to go. When I hear "The Time is Here, The Time is Now", I still wince at the thought of singing it over and over again in that studio in London, throughout the day and into the night, with the same torture again the next day. It seemed to go on forever, and when Mr Smith was happy with the final take, it sounded no different to me than the first.

There was a fair amount of tanking going on in and around the studio. We loaded up our spirits when they would flag with spirits out of bottles, and there were some nights when the final take would be something of a mystery to my ears upon hearing it at the next session.

When it was finally recorded and mixed, we took the unusual step, for the time, of putting it in a sleeve that had been designed in keeping with the concept. There wasn't the usual cover with a photograph of the artist but, instead, an image of dead doves, which had been killed by someone, using them as ashtrays for stubbing out their cigarettes. The artist won an award somewhere for this imagery, and the absurdity of the picture was intended to convey the horror of war. Not in any realistic, offensive way, mind you, but in this rather more profound, arty-farty kind of fashion. It was important, thought the moguls, not to deter the buying public from reaching for it; important not to scare them.

The album was launched at the Concert for Peace in the library of the RDS in Dublin on November 11, 1970, Armistice Day. Oliver, or The Captain, as he was known, really pushed the boat out for one of the biggest concerts the city had seen in ages.

We performed it to an audience of politicians from North and South of the border, priests, bishops, vicars and two rabbis. The great and the good from showbiz, press, the world of sports, TV and radio, all swept the evening to levels of emotion seldom matched in concerts I'd ever been to. Terry Wogan was compère, The RTÉ Light Orchestra, conducted by Don Gold, provided the backing, and Hilton Edwards did the narration. Edwards was Mac Liammóir's partner and the great man himself couldn't make the launch because his sight was failing and he needed an operation.

At rehearsal the night before, I hadn't been there to hear this newcomer's contribution, and on the evening of the performance I offered him a swig from a bottle of napper I was using to calm him down. I thought he looked a bit nervous. What nerve, I was later to discover, but the man had a decent gulp, nonetheless.

The concert was a terrific occasion. Everyone believed it was a seminal moment in Irish music, with the merging of two hitherto separate strands, pop and classical. The complimentary reviews said so the next day and things looked good for this unusual package.

But it went nowhere fast. Actually, it went straight downhill in the UK. I don't believe the record company spent a shilling promoting it and someone, somewhere, in the CBS organisation in London obviously concluded that it was a non-starter.

Once again, the beach girls on Bondi were not going to be worried by the Freshmen.

There was a tragic footnote to that big gala concert in the RDS. After an all-night party, celebrating its success, the stage manager, Joe O'Sullivan, was killed in a crash just a few hundred yards from his home. It was a tragic end to a young and talented life, a violent end that cast a cloud on us all.

I was drinking with Billy in the Four Courts Bar on the Quays a few days later, and the conversation went something like this.

"Big night then, Billy. What'd you make of it all?"

"Load of shite, head," was the abrupt reply and, to tell the truth, I wasn't surprised. He truly was a hard man to please and while I was content to be a bit cynical about the whole peace business and the chance of a collection of songs having even the slightest effect, I believed the actual event was a major turning point in the life of the band.

Bill was having none of it. He had other things on his mind anyway, but he never really supported the venture with anything like his normal enthusiasm. It was the creative vacuum that I believe repelled him, and the feel of the project never made it into his heart. He was built for better things, and singing other men's original songs, when they weren't members of the band, didn't appeal.

We performed the Peace Concert on a couple of occasions after the RDS in smaller venues around the country. There was one famous occasion that stays in my mind and I'm sure is remembered by many others, for slightly different reasons. This was the only night that Mac Liammóir appeared live and it happened in the Oratory in UCD, Dublin.

A famous priest, Fr Peyton, he of "the family that prays together, stays together" fame, was in attendance and the place was, once again, packed with all kinds of serious churchmen. Not at all like the screaming ladies of Dublin and Cork, but much the same in every other way. I was hoping that the student's chapel, which had been cleared of its seating and religious ornaments, wouldn't begin to rumble or vibrate when certain members of the band appeared, but I needn't have worried; all went well and the place remained calm. Mac Liammóir was nearly blind, but like the legend he was insisted on doing the show at least once in his life. He loved it and the setting was an ideal theatre for his mellifluent tones.

After the gig, Yvonne and one of my neighbours, the lady who had saved my life with the whiskey, invited a gaggle of priests back to our place for a few bevvies. There was a good vibe in the air, and a drinks party with the holy men was a good excuse to keep it going. A few lads from the band came back as well, and the booze flowed for hours. The lounge of the house in Terenure had never seen so many men in black, all enthralled by the beautiful Yvonne, who probably wasn't aware of the serious effect she was having on them. Or there again, maybe she was.

A couple of hours later, and the festivities weren't showing any signs of winding up, when it entered my befuddled brain that a bit of *craic* was needed in the proceedings; something that would test their mettle.

I was thinking of the shotgun that Billy had left under the bed after a day's shooting a couple of nights before. It was unloaded, of course, but they weren't to know that.

Steadying myself at the top of the stairs, I began the descent, clearing my throat loudly and with the gun barrel opened over my arm, shouted at the top of my slurring voice, as I cocked it at the bottom of the stairs, "Every fuckin' Catholic outta here."

And this after the Peace Concert. Holy God, you never saw a place empty as quick. The holy men raced to the door, ignoring my bleary-eyed assurances that I was only taking the piss. Lots of hurried goodbyes, we'll meet again stuff, but there was no stopping them and it was an icy place they closed the door on. I had let everyone down again, and it was an enraged wife and neighbour who were left in the judgment seat. I was condemned, of course, one more time to the doghouse. But the gigs kept coming.

It was both a great thrill and, as time wore on, an unrelenting threat, to stand on the same stage as Mr Brown. Whether singing, saxing, playing piano, harmonising, or sharing a drink, this man could do it better than anyone I'd ever encountered.

As our crowds grew bigger and more frantic, as the girls began to scream our names before we appeared on stage, I used to listen to what name was being shouted the loudest. I still had it in my head that as I was the only one not to play an instrument, I was meant to be the main attraction. It wouldn't do me any good if the blond bombshell became the biggest in the band. What would I do? Fuck that for a game of soldiers.

We were big drinking buddies and he was content to share the spotlight with me, but I couldn't quite believe that that was as far as it would go. I had visions of me being turfed out, a miserable failure, an outcast, a plonker, and I drank all the harder to drown these worries. I was envious of the man's ability; I couldn't match up. He was a superb singer, whereas I was a ball waver. And after that, I didn't see anything else to warrant me standing in front of this master and hogging the limelight. More and more, I needed strong drink to get up at all. Whereas before I had never hesitated to run onto any stage and sing my head off, now I needed liquid help to get over all the hang-ups and hangovers I carried around with me.

Notwithstanding this growing paranoia, it was impossible to work with the man and not, on at least a couple of occasions nightly, be spellbound by his gifts. We shared magazine covers, radio shows, TV interviews and made over twenty singles and three albums together, and only on the rarest of occasions could I find fault with his generous soul. He would be the first to stand aside in the limelight stakes, and this added to his greatness. His was a true gift to the business and he shared his talents with all.

And we sacked him.

FIFTEEN

Sacking the Star

With growing problems in his personal life, it was impossible to predict what the man would do next. He began to miss gigs, incurring a mighty wrath from us, less-talented but slightly more righteous souls. There was a limit you were not meant to exceed and Billy went over it on a regular basis.

Collectively we spoke to him and some of the brethren tried to help him, individually, as well. But there was a reluctance to overstep the mark. When a man's marriage is breaking down, and there is another love in the background, it greatly limits your ability to intervene. It's doubtful anyway that any of us would have had the skills needed to help him effectively through this time in his journey. We didn't give him the time or the back-up needed to face the enormity of what he was deciding. He lacked the ability to let us know that this was just a phase, that he would be OK when it was over, that his future really lay with us. There were no time-outs in those hectic days, just the lure of the bright lights and all the attendant glitter, plus, of course, the rolls of money.

It's been said that anything goes in showbusiness; that people don't judge you and the reason for that, is that everyone is so concerned with themselves that they don't even see what's happening.

I was saddened to see him in such trouble, and to witness his anguish over the future. Three children were involved and, as far as I could fathom, his guilt over this was killing him. Mahon and I tried to stick up for him as long as possible, but the situation just kept getting worse. So it was goodbye Billy, hello Ivan, Ivan Laybourne.

But it wasn't as simple as that. The day we sacked our musical maestro was the beginning of the end for us all, or rather that particular group of Freshmen. We would continue to pack ballrooms all over the country, but there was a sense that we were always proving that we could do without him. We continued recording and, in fact, came up with possibly the greatest pop record the band ever made, "Swannee River", a stunning display of Laybourne's arranging talent. It's strange to relate that after getting shot of the marvel that was Brown we would make a record that gained rave reviews not only here, but in the States as well. Even stranger was that Ivan came from Larne, like Bill, and he would be the first to agree that his predecessor had influenced his development as a musician.

Music wasn't the only talent young Laybourne possessed. He was quite a looker and the ladies were all too willing to investigate his charm. He was also up for adventure and one evening on the train to Cork will never be forgotten.

We were playing in Cork and I had arranged to meet him in the Aisling Hotel, which was handily situated for the main road south. The other minstrels had gone on ahead and the drinking session started off innocently enough, if that can be said about two serious men taking the stuff on board. Round followed round and soon the thoughts of driving to Cork in daylight traffic became more and more of a major turn-off. When the barman informed us that the simplest remedy was to take the train, which departed at six from just over the way, our minds were made up. This made sense. We could arrange a taxi at the far end and come back with the lads.

Staggering down the platform, by now well oiled, I caught sight of a most beautifully rounded backside, gently pushing her luggage onto the shelf overhead in the first-class carriage. We were shuffling our way down to the third-class compartment, but this inviting vision changed all that.

"In here, Ivan," I shouted. "This is where we are."

And two fairly sozzled, horny musicians sat down facing this very, very attractive young woman. She was about 25 years old and appeared full of confidence in her ability to deal with the two intruders who had just invaded her solitude for the trip southwards.

The eagle-eyed ticket collector, having spotted our actions in bettering our passage, insisted we pay the extra tariff, which we gladly did.

As the train chugged out of Heuston Station, I

was beside myself with devilment and it was obvious that Mr Laybourne was eagerly plotting as well. There was an air of semi-dementia as we slowly made speed, and my mind was desperately trying to work out a suitable approach and, at the same time, how not to blow the opening lines that might lead God knows where with this sophisticated lady.

I should mention that the carriage was of the old-fashioned type. It was a self-contained compartment with sliding doors opening onto a corridor. The three of us sat in total silence.

"Would you like to dance?"

It just came out of my mouth. And it was such a ridiculous question that it took her by surprise as well.

"But there's no music," was all she came back with, a statement that proved to be her Waterloo. When I heard this mildest of protestations, I knew immediately that this truly was a fellow-traveller, a day-tripper par excellence, and the serpent struggled to clear his drunken head.

"No problem," was my immediate celebratory reply. "My buddy will sing."

Laybourne obliged and began rendering a fairly passable version of the Johnny Ray classic "Cry" as the beautiful damsel and myself took the floor, swaying as the choo-choo wound its merry way.

And fair play to Ivan. It wasn't what you could call an everyday happening on a train, but the Larne warbler kept it going long enough for the romance to blossom, as we trundled on towards the Lee and the hungry reptile made a most welcome appearance about halfway through the trip. Not in the carriage of course, but in one of the toilets.

Her appetite and attitude seemed to be "in for a penny, in for a pound" and the well-equipped first-class lover took her pleasure with my semi-comatose partner as well. Needless to say, I don't recall the gig, just the journey.

Oliver knew it would be nigh on impossible to replace our mainstay, but believed that there was enough talent to make a considerable living and remain in the top ten bands, at least. But when we ganged up on Maurice Henry, some time after we had dismissed Billy, he sensed that the mighty band was fast running out of time.

He had taken us as far as it was possible to go in Ireland. We packed halls in the major cities and towns throughout the land and quite a few rural areas as well. There wasn't a show we hadn't appeared on, several times, and he had pushed us to the limit in the quest to broaden our appeal further. Years before Billy's departure, we had ceased wearing suits and the casual look, the well-thought-out, off-the-cuff style was our norm. Oliver encouraged us, at every turn, to be different and there were no shortage of takers. The man was not a quitter and there was no hint of throwing in the towel, but I had the feeling that his dream for this particular band had faded. He managed several acts and promoted major concerts all over the country, so he didn't spend time agonising about our future. Henceforth, we would become just another money stream in the organisation; profitable for sure, but one of limited potential.

The *Peace on Earth* album had sounded the death knell for Maurice, because, through the policy adopted by the record company, our bandleader played no part in it. The "Jim Reeves syndrome" claimed another scalp. He'll have to go, was the sentiment and his role in keeping the whole business together wasn't considered important in our rebellious, short-sighted eyes. With Ivan playing guitar and Mahon having practically abandoned the trombone and trumpet, there was little or no brass section and our founder was more or less reduced to "stepping" to the music.

The showband steps were as big a part of the scene as the band snaps. A little hop forward with your left foot, cross over with the right, and a sprightly skip back to where you started. It was a joke in the beginning, but it became addictive. Depending on the tempo of the song, and the state of inebriation, it was touch and go if you could do it at all. Sean could do it like a Spanish nobleman, expressing himself in flamenco, using his trumpet as castanets. His rhythmic feet beat time like a gifted señor, and there were nights you felt like tripping him up, especially if he was singing into the same mike as yourself, when you weren't even meant to be stepping, and you, leery eyed with the sauce. It could make a man dizzy and all the while, he'd be smiling the "I have you now, Bigman, beat this" smile.

The band without Maurice developed into a type of mod-pop outfit, releasing a couple of minor hits on CBS, written by ourselves and performed by Ivan and Davy. There was the usual block harmony, but the axis of attack was now definitely in the hands of the aforementioned duo. Damien and Torry were happy with this arrangement, but I was all at sea and could see no future for myself in the new dispensation. One of the main promoters in the west of Ireland, Joe O'Neill, used to categorise the bands in the following fashion: country-pop and mod-pop, and he had us definitely in the last category. But unlike this ex-cathedra pronouncement from the west, there was no room for wild men in our new culture and I knew that was how I was seen.

But I wasn't wild; I was just clinging on, drinking my fears away and doing the best I could to bluff my way through when I got to the gig. I lived in Dublin and rarely travelled in the bus with the rest of them, and sometimes I would find myself driving home, not too sure where I was coming back from. Sean told me years later that they wanted to sack me, but Oliver, for some reason, cautioned against it and insisted I had a role to play. At the time, I didn't see it and was what could reasonably be described as a most unhappy chappy.

The trouble in the North had erupted and widespread rioting and gunfire had made our journeys at night time very precarious. It was no place for a band of musicians carrying large sums of money late at night. It was never discussed much at the time, but a few of them were under severe pressure from wives and families to quit and make a crust elsewhere. It was a bad time for a divided band and our outfit was ruptured in many places, like drinks culture, political culture, musical culture and just about any culture you could imagine. It was not a band with a future.

Out of the blue, Davy and Damien announced they were leaving. The timing of the news was a genuine surprise, but I have to say I wasn't disappointed. Our guitarist was heading off to South Africa to begin afresh with his brother and friend, singing songs under the name of The Blarney Brothers.

Davy wasn't joining another outfit, but he had lived enough of a nightmare to take steps to keep his own show on the road. I recall a rather testy conversation we had before his departure. We agreed that we had been friends, but that now, mainly due to my crazy drinking, the fire had gone out. He blamed me for wrecking a great band, and suggested strongly that I do something about it or kiss the music goodbye.

"Goodnight, God bless and safe home to you too," I mused. It was easy to dismiss his righteousness as just a sad man's rant, but in truth, he was a powerful man. He had seen his dreams ruined by madness and was now doing the only thing left open to him. I wasn't privy to his plans, and he certainly had no intentions of sharing them with me, but now we were four. Bondi Beach was further away than ever.

We auditioned for a new stickman in the Floral Hall one afternoon before a gig in the Boom-Boom Room in Cornmarket, Belfast. The venue was managed by young Sammy Smyth, he of the long defunct Pentagon Promotions fame, and it was provided free of charge to old buddies. It also housed the Zoo and Sammy had the responsibility of ensuring that all went according to plan in this one-time major tourist attraction.

We had advertised in the local papers and the small scene in the North was well aware the Freshmen were on the lookout for a drummer. We arranged to audition about half a dozen, and what was left of the band set up and began the hopeful quest. I had a bottle of strong, black, Northern whiskey in my case and visited it several times during the afternoon. Sounds weren't exactly creating waves across the Lagan, as I drifted up to see Sammy in his office upstairs.

He was in top form and we passed the firewater back and forth across his desk. With a glint of devilment in his eyes, he invited me to accompany him on a visit to see the masturbating monkeys of Belfast Zoo.

They sat in a row on the branch of a tree and with their tiny hands, they pulled their little willies. It was a sight to see and I swear they were all smiling. Chug, chug, tug, tug, grinning from ear to ear, they stared out at the two frenzied men who looked on in wondrous awe.

All thoughts of the selection process going on back inside the hall were forgotten at the sight of this hilarious activity. The wanking apes, the much needed whiskey and the mind-blowing tobacco we'd shared in his office, had deflected my attention from the task at hand, and by the time I arrived back at the scene, the deed had been done. Lindsay Looney, formerly of the College Boys, had been selected as our new drummer. I couldn't get the sight of the horny monkeys out of my head and wasn't in much of a position to celebrate or otherwise.

Sammy took me to his home on the outskirts of the city for a meal and my mind was floating between two different constellations when he reminded me of the gig in the Boom-Boom. Once again, I had forgotten about it completely and soon found myself riding a mushroom into Belfast.

I was sat on its back, right up at the crown and it was a massive, bloody thing. I was holding on for dear life and held the leather reins in my hands, which were guiding it through the streets of Belfast. It was propelled by hundreds of tiny legs, and it took real skill to get them to turn in the same direction all at the same time.

Then, suddenly, I was sitting beside a taxi-driver, asking why he had bought a mushroom instead of a car. What's the big idea, I wanted to know, and before he replied, I was back atop the flying fungus, making tracks to the gig.

I gingerly foot-clouded my way up the narrow stairs of the club. Mahon saw me and came over and asked if I was OK. His head kept turning from mushroom to flesh and back again. My feet were somewhere in disappearing space as he guided me to the small dressing room with instructions to lie down and rest.

If Davy was playing that night, if it was his farewell to the band, then it was a fitting one. I didn't appear. I was trying to get out of the mushroom.

As Damien closed the door on his Freshmen career to head for Africa, he opened it for another guitar man who would play a major role in the remaining life of the band. This man is remembered by many as the only guitarist we ever had, so great was his contribution in the 1970s, and he became one of the major driving forces in the third incarnation of the Freshmen.

The first band had been a singer out front, three brass, two guitar, mixum-gatherum, jack-of-all-trades showband. A thrill to sing in front of, with a tightness that could push you beyond your edge. It played with an unforgettable passion and spread its energy through the heart of every man, woman and priest who ever heard it. It featured Billy, with all his young, raw, unforgiving talent and beauty. There was a hope that we could become the best. And there was every chance with such a genius at the helm.

The second outfit was the one that broke all the records. It had exactly the same personnel, but the music had changed. This band sang harmony, with enough power to lift you off your feet. Its five voices sang anything from the Beatles to Bach to the Beach Boys, all in a magical flowing blend. It sang the Bourrée No. 2 from the English Suite in B minor as fluently as "Good Vibrations", and it put together an arrangement of "Yesterday" that amazed its author, Paul McCartney. That version of the band set attendance records in halls throughout the land and appeared on every major TV show in the British Isles. Whereas there was an aspiration to be the best in the earlier journey, this lot believed they were just that. It was a thrill, a joy, an honour, a threat, a danger, a challenge, an enricher, a menace and, ultimately, an addictive seducer.

The expectant wake took a long time, but before death could be pronounced and a certificate issued, the wonderful, aforementioned Tiger Taylor appeared to revive the corpse. David Walter Taylor was a son of working-class Belfast, a man so gifted on his instrument that the great Jimi Hendrix counted him a friend. He played his way to stardom with a band in the early 1960s called Eire Apparent and attracted rave reviews with his song "Rock and Roll Band", which broke the Top 100 in America but, with no promotion, floundered. He had toured Europe with the American guitar icon, and the group made such an impression that Hendrix produced a couple of tracks on their one-and-only album *Sunrise*. There was no doubt that Tiger knew what it was all about.

He got on well with the other men but, as he and I travelled together from Dublin to the gigs nationwide, a new spirit of madness was born. There was an urge to do it all over again, and it was shared by the man with the head of hair that would have rivalled Luke Kelly's in his heyday. There was only one Tiger and we set targets and dreamed dreams in the motor, en route to work, that nearly came off. The plan was simple; get Billy back and, with a few little changes here and there, there was no limit to what we could achieve. Mind you, we took a lot of the hard stuff when discussing our plans, but you wouldn't mind that, it was showbusiness, after all.

Poor Ivan was between a rock and a hard place. We wanted him to stay and work with Bill, but he had separate plans and moved on with his life. He had enjoyed the mad ride and wasn't what you could describe as a reluctant passenger, like some of the other, older guys, and years later during a reunion gig he explained his belief that in showbusiness, to get to the top, it was a man's duty to leave no turn unstoned. And we had certainly tried to do just that.

Tiger had played with Billy before in the Billy Brown Superband, and with the Brown O'Brien Band, so it was with bated breath and Oliver's blessing that I called my ex-partner in Canada, where he was touring with the Brown O'Brien Band, and invited him to return.

I had heard on the grapevine that he wasn't too

happy in North America and was beside myself with
joy when he said he was on for it. He flew home to
Dublin a couple of days later, leaving the other guys
behind, and we celebrated his return with a night in
a pub in the city. We talked the talk all night long,
and it was like all my birthdays came together to be
in his company again.

He had written some great songs whilst in the
North American colony and was raring to have a go
at the Irish scene once again. We rehearsed for a week
in the west of Ireland, and opened phase three of the
Freshmen towards the end of the practice with a gig
in a local hall. The night went well enough to evince
hope that it might happen again, but it was well
short of a real storm. We now had two keyboards,
one of them supplied by a young enthusiast from
Newtownards, Raymond Donnan, who also blew
sax, and along with Tiger, Torry, Lindsay, and Sean,
the mercury was rising.

There were now two distinct camps, one in the
North and the other based in Dublin, and there was
a deal of tension, shall we say, between them. Torry
normally drove the Northern contingent to the gigs,
and I looked after the transport of the Southern-
based brethren. One particular night highlights the
difficulty we were experiencing.

It was a time of secret resentments. Instead of
coming straight out and saying what was on your
mind, the usual practice was to drop hints and
behave in a fashion that was guaranteed to incense
the offending party. It's the same in all organisations,
and we were no different than most, but the public
outcome of these vendettas was, sometimes,
memorable.

Even at the best of times, I had become used to high tension between guys who were sick to the teeth putting up with each other's unacceptable foibles – for example, a mini fist-fight in the dressing corridor, before going onstage in Crosshaven. It was what it was, a stress-buster, and there was never any follow-up to such outbursts, but one night in Tullamore, it was different.

We got there early to rehearse, and some of the lads went on the piss. Now, as any drinker knows, there are nights you can take it, and then there are times when, even half of what you normally use can put you away in the head. Sean, although living in the North, was definitely in the Southern camp of serious drinking men who were prone to rush their intake before a gig would start.

On this particular evening, the Downpatrick singer was the worse for wear and the crowd was treated to mike feedback of that high, screeching, eardrum piercing type. It was Sean's job to set the levels, so, in the middle of the first number, with a couple of men trying their best to put on a show for the rows of onlookers, Megahy crossed the stage to adjust the amplifier and settle the howl. It worked and now it was possible to continue singing and actually hear yourself. But Sean was having none of it. Like a flash, he went back to the power amp and reset the levers. Whine, whine, howl, screech, scream, shriek and any other offensive buzz you can imagine. All I could do was laugh, but the enraged bassman took off his beautiful and expensive Fender, and launched it across at the bedazzled dancing sound chief, just missing our innocent drummer, Lindsay. It made a perfect accompaniment to the howling mikes as it hit the ground, because it was still plugged into its own amplifier. Jaysus, the crowd stared up in a state of amazement. This must be rock 'n' roll, seemed to be their reaction, because they loved it. Megahy walked right off the stage into his car and drove home to Ballymena.

There was no bad word from the promoter at the end of the night, and he paid up without fuss. We retired to the hotel to have a drink and thrash the matter out. The Southern warriors were highly offended at Megahy's desertion and righteous words were uttered.

Oliver arrived the next day to speak to us about the drinking and with a warning that things would have to improve on the sobriety front, or he might have second thoughts about remaining as manager.

Poor Lindsay had had enough. He valued his life and sanity a lot more than the wages we were offering and quit soon after, to be replaced by John Wilson, ex-drummer with Taste. Wilson travelled with our roadie, John Rogers, known to all as Harpo, to gigs in the van, and so I never really got to know the man. I knew he was a drummer of renown and enjoyed his solos that always pulled the house down. I inevitably listened to them when swigging from a bottle of something or other stashed near the stage. We had a rule that you couldn't bring the booze onto the bandstand; it would have sent out the wrong message. It was all right to stagger around it, but you daren't allow the paying customers to watch the actual engorgement.

Within a short while, Megahy had decided to run up the white flag. He could take no more and life on the road was becoming more and more dangerous. He had to drive home after every gig and criss-crossed dangerous tracts of land, not knowing who'd be out on dark manoeuvres. And besides, the band, for the first time, was based in Dublin and this change made it even more awkward for him, particularly as an unpredictable chap like myself was leading it. Tensions were high all over and his departure came as no great surprise. We missed his great playing.

Speaking of dangerous driving conditions, it is with a genuine sense of remorse that I describe what it was like driving during those desperate times.

The only night I ever had a serious accident – the time I met the horse in Horse and Jockey – I was stone-cold sober. But for the next decade and a half, I drove the highways and byways of Ireland, North and South, with no regard for other road-users' safety, my passengers' or my own. There were nights when I would leave Kerry and wake up halfway to Dublin, still behind the wheel, and wonder how I'd got so far. I wouldn't remember whole journeys, like the trip down the turnpike in Boston, and despite vowing to myself that I wouldn't repeat this madness, the very next night I'd do the same again.

There were times when the garda patrol car would stop the car and, on seeing it was a band, they'd tell you what bands were on the road ahead of you and ask if there was any chance you'd have a drop in the car. I left many a checkpoint with a huge sigh of relief and with an emptier bottle of vodka. Most journeys began in apprehension, when I would collect Tiger at his house, and the first thing he would say would be: "Remember talking to the law last night, Bigman? You were in some state."

I think he used to do it to terrorise me, as the question was asked nearly every night. It was torture, and the insanity of it all, the real madness, was that I knew that, no matter what promises I'd made to others, the same lunacy was on the way. There was a bewildering confusion and a demoralisation about it all, but I never thought of stopping the drink, only of cutting down.

But it wasn't always plain-sailing with the boys in blue. One day, a friend from London, a duty officer with Aer Lingus, rang my home before midday. We started a session and were genuinely drunk when tea-time came and we ate a bite before heading to Dungannon in County Tyrone for an 11 o'clock start.

We had arranged to meet a friend of his and when we picked up this chap, I bought two bottles of whiskey for the trip. One of them was practically gone, when I rammed the car into a bridge about twenty miles south of the venue, and reversed from the crash site without even stopping to examine the damage. The object was to get there on time, and I instructed my ossified pal to look out the window to see and hear if the tyre was rubbing against the car's frame. That being the case, then we would stop. It wasn't and we kept moving.

That gig is just another of many blurred evenings, but I remember heading back to the city, and being so disgusted with the damage done to the front of the car that we drank the other bottle of juice on the way home.

I was arrested in Dublin for driving on the footpath and was taken in the back of a garda car to the station. The breathalyzer had been in operation for a few years, but at this particular time its use was temporarily suspended due to a pending appeal against its constitutionality.

"Are you drunk?" the station sarge demanded.

"No."

"What day of the week is it?"

I was totally flummoxed.

"I know there're seven of them. It could be any one," was the only reply I could muster.

At that, another sergeant arrived in the barracks to begin duty and he recognised me as one of the bandsmen who had recently performed for the old folks' Christmas party in the city's biggest garda station.

I got off with a major bollicking and the strange passenger who had journeyed to Dungannon and back with scarcely a word volunteered to drive me home and make sure I didn't have access to the car before I'd sobered up. Amazed that he could speak, never mind drive, I waited until we were safely out of sight of the cop shop and then demanded the keys and put him out on the side of the street. It was hardly the gesture of a grateful man.

The same thing happened a couple of weeks later, and this time I ended up in the drunk-tank in the Four Courts. I was bailed to appear on a charge of drunken and dangerous driving, but that didn't stop me. It didn't seem possible to stop. I mean, of course it was possible to stop for a couple of weeks; I'd done it many times. But to approach it as a problem, accept it as a major stumbling block, which would take me out of the picture if I didn't; that was a different matter. How in Jaysus could a man sing in a band and not drink? That would have been completely impossible. There was a lot more madness to come.

"Could you not wait until after the gig, and then drink your heads off?" I remember the Captain asking. He was genuinely mystified and bemused by it all, as he didn't drink himself and couldn't understand the liquor imperative that traps a man in its wake.

One of the last major gigs for Megahy was a TV show in Spain to celebrate the first colour broadcast by TVE, the national broadcaster. But before the three-day fiesta in Madrid, more sacking was in the air. We gave Mr Wilson his marching orders, primarily for his love of good books. John was an amazing drummer to listen to as he rocked the roof off ballrooms all over the country, but it was a bit irritating for the rest of the brethren, particularly Brother Brown, when he would take out a novel and read it during the slower numbers. It was just a small thing, but as I have already alluded to, once a band begins firing men there's no knowing where it will end. At any rate, exit John, enter Paddy. Paddy Freeney, the last permanent drummer who would ever sit behind the skins and beat the shit out of whatever drums sat in front of him.

In the studio in Spain, he started with a kit that could have been used at Franco's wedding party. There was the biggest bass drum any of us had ever seen, and the one cymbal was roughly the size of a shitake mushroom. Our job was to mime three Freshmen oldies, including "Papa oo Mow Mow", and in hindsight, it was to prove a continental farewell party for our Ballymena bassman. It was very different to any TV work we had experienced before, and the main one was the bar in the studio.

We arrived for an early-morning work schedule, heads wrecked and slightly disoriented from the previous nights intake, dying for a cure and there in front of our delighted eyes was a fully-serviced drinks area, right there in the corner of the Madrid film set. It had been used to make the Clint Eastwood *For a Few Dollars More* series of films and there was every type of head-wrecking liquid you could dream of.

"O viva España", for sure – this nation knew how to make television programmes. It was like a visit to Lourdes for the cure. Thus was the scene set for a sauce carnival that few working bands had ever known, in a television studio at least. We drank the place dry.

In between shots with a troupe of gorgeous dancers, we hurried to the refreshment area to nurse the buzz and, just maybe, nudge it that little bit higher.

If Freeney didn't know what he was letting himself in for at Dublin Airport the previous day, when he joined up, then he had a fair old clue as he sat behind the giant kit and looked on as Brown and I stood singing "Papa oo" over a garden wall, looking out at the pirouetting body of dancers, with our trousers dropped. I don't recall if we were free-ballin' Freshmen or if we were righteously clad, but the atmosphere was one of enormous glee.

The two beautiful female presenters wore these great big animal heads. One was a monkey and the other a horse, and we couldn't understand the imagery. But what matter, we had business at the bar. Somehow or other we got the thing done, and I've often wondered what the Spanish kids thought of it all, if it was ever transmitted.

One that was broadcast, and much commented upon, was an appearance on a show on RTÉ television. I got a call from Oliver's office one morning, asking if I knew how to sing "Oh Carol", the old Paul Anka hit. It was explained that Joe Dolan had been scheduled and a backing track recorded for his voice, and would I go out to the studios in Donnybrook and see if it was a runner. If not, they'd have to get someone else.

Joe sings somewhere between tenor and the sky and my offerings were normally bass to baritone, but the lure of the old fame drug told my hungry head that it was grand. The key was fine, even though it was hurting my left ball to reach for some of the notes.

"It'll be dead on when I have a few more scoops," I said to myself, as the amount already down was just the normal start-up quota. There was a bottle in the dressing room, and I gave it a bit of a lashing before going back to the next rehearsal and, indeed, the voice had improved quite a bit. In hindsight, it probably wasn't my singing that had gotten better, more likely my ear had been sweetened by the booze, but I was convinced that whatever key Joe could manage, I could do as well. And the whiskey was telling me, probably a lot better too.

The script would have read something as follows: "musical backing begins, cut to singer leaning casually on juke-box, and then track him as he begins to sing and walk down the steps, to the dance floor." The stairway to be negotiated wasn't too steep and during the first couple of runs, presented no problem.

When the bottle was finished, it struck me that the one in the boot of my car would be needed, just to make the thing spot on, and when I couldn't find the car where I'd left it I called security. I also gave Paddy Freeney a call and, explaining the rotten luck about the motor, asked him to bring over a bottle of something from the pub he owned.

The security staff were taking details from a slightly confused Paul Anka sound-alike when Paddy whispered that he had just seen the car parked outside in the park, and, mightily embarrassed, we repaired to the changing area and I took a few hefty swigs from the relief bottle.

I think I started the song OK and came in where I was meant to, but my ambulatory skills on the descent proved another matter. I was in the middle of the opening line of the ditty, exclaiming to Carol what a fool I was, when one foot sort of kicked the other and thrust me forward in a rush to the bottom. Miraculously, I didn't fall, but the show was live and the viewers at home had a ball.

Once again, Mr Karma was sitting in the corner of the studio making copious notes, and he made a special memo when the producer of the show, another Strabane man, John McColgan, assured me, as the credits rolled, that I'd never sing on RTÉ again. I was too smashed to care, but there was a cool vibe for a couple of days afterwards, with the office. As I mentioned earlier, thoughts alone do not produce Mr Karma, only actions. Negative or unskilful remorse and fear are the ripening tools of his grand design. He never missed a trick.

Big Skins had lost the knack of swing,
Just kept on boozin' and losin'
Sunk too far down to turn around
He'd gone too far, in the wrong direction.

SIXTEEN

Reality Bites

It got to the point where my long-suffering wife could take no more. She had pleaded with me for years to sober up and looked on as the situation deteriorated. There was no telling where it would end; when, if ever, I would grow up and start acting like a human being, a man.

She was sickened by years of disappointment, disrespect, violent outbursts and everything else that accompanies insanity. I was shell-shocked when she announced her decision to leave and take the two girls with her, to set up home again in America. Up to this juncture, I had led a charmed life, with only minor scars compared to most men, but this news made me sick.

Little did she know the wise decision she was making, for, by now, and for some time before her move to freedom, the terrible nightmares that I was entertaining, almost nightly, placed her and the kids in mortal danger.

The mad adventures were a part of the drink-fuelled escape, like a lingering death wish that wouldn't go away. Like driving blind drunk at one hundred miles an hour, in the middle of the night, too drunk even to see the speedometer and laughing crazily as Tiger counted the speed until we reached the ton. He was minding the speedo, I was minding the road, and God was minding us both.

But as I sat on nights off in the house in Terenure, looking into the granite fireplace, awaiting the nightly appearance of the elephants and the rats with big heads, I knew the real meaning of despair. Yvonne would be asleep in bed, as I held vigil for the faces in the sparkling stone, and I used to dare them to appear, shouting out that I wasn't afraid. Often, I was disappointed if they didn't show before the drink vanished, and was always checking the levels of whatever piss I'd be supping. I believed it was the mark of a true drinking man not to be worried about seeing these horrors, but to adopt a macho attitude and show them who was boss. This, I imagined, was what a real warrior would do.

My twisted soul was telling me that life was foul and the living of it rotten. The world was a terrible place and the two little girls, asleep upstairs with their mother, didn't deserve to grow up in such a stinking reality. I loved them too much to allow this to happen, but what could I do about it, and when could it be done?

These were the darkest days of my life. I found that if the drink was running out too fast, a trip to the toilet and a sip of disinfectant would burn the temples with a fire that made them pulse with a red heat. Not too much for there was always the danger of a Vesuvian eruption and that, even to a horribly drunk man, was unacceptable.

The unthinkable was entertained but, thankfully, to whatever God that rules, the nightmare never got any further than my sick imaginings.

Before Yvonne left, she did something that saved my life, and for which I shall always be in her debt. She made contact with a couple of men who came to my home to talk to me about alcoholism. I didn't avail of their help immediately, but the time was approaching fast.

I stood alone at the big bay window in Dublin airport, and watched the clouds close in on the plane, taking Yvonne, Sinead and Sorca, to a new life in Baltimore, Maryland. My heart was breaking as tears flooded my eyes and ran out of my soul. I couldn't think about anything other than my death, but was such a coward I hadn't a hope of doing it. I believed this was the end, the dismal denouement of a wasted life. There was no anger in me, just a sense of desperate loss, for I knew that this was the end of my life with my wife and two little girls. I'd been a right failure as a husband and father, but I still loved them all.

At the time, there was a circular bar in the observation area at the airport. I had been off the drink for a few weeks, hoping that some miracle would happen and maybe things might, somehow, be put right, but at this moment, I was very aware that, simply by turning around, I would find the answer to my problem. I'd drink myself to death, no mistake.

Just as I turned to the bar, two men came towards me with their hands out. It was my brothers, Eugene and Gerry, who had travelled down from Strabane, to be with me and say goodbye to the girls.

"They're gone, lads, let's have a drink."

"Not for us, Derek, and not for you either, c'mon, we're getting outta here," was the unanimous reply and, for some reason, we repaired to the empty house which had been sold but as yet unoccupied by the new owner. It was a stupid place to go, but there was some strange undercurrent at work, drawing me back, as it were, to the scene of the loss.

We stayed together that night, and I will never forget the kindness shown by those two men to their brother during his real hour of need.

And the band played on.

SEVENTEEN

Mr Karma Strikes

Men and boys were coming and going in the band so often, it was hard to keep up with them. We were crossing and recrossing the border at night and there was a dreadful sense of danger in the air, when, in July 1975, the Miami tragedy happened. Three innocent men were slaughtered in a most callous fashion just north of Newry, as they drove home from a gig in Banbridge, and the world was shocked at the atrocity. Fran O'Toole, Brian McCoy and Stephen Travers were killed by Loyalist paramilitaries parading as legitimate soldiers, and the massacre incensed the nation. It frightened the life out of all working bands as well, and we had a big book in the North.

We were all based in Dublin except for Mahon, and by now travelling across the border was a real chilling experience. I remember one night, when a couple of us were in the van along with our roadie, a mighty man from Meath by the name of Gerry Crinnion, when we spotted a wire trailing across the road, sticking out from the side of a hedge. The Meath man had balls of steel, but he pulled the Transit up immediately. It was a byroad in South Armagh, as we had been detoured from the main Newry line because of a bomb scare.

We must have fired stones at the cable for about an hour, sometimes hitting it, but with no result. If it had been a bomb, we would have been blown to kingdom come, but that thought didn't seem to register. We had to make the gig. We needed the money and had travelled too far to turn back. We reversed the van back down the road and, with all hands holding our collective breath, drove over the offending article at top speed.

There were nightmare runs through Belfast, late at night, with nobody on the streets except the odd soldier and, at those times, it was anybody's guess what was going to happen or where. Sometimes the van was pulled apart by the security forces and, the odd time, we were stopped and questioned by the paramilitaries.

I remember speeding out of the Bogside in Derry late one night after a gig there, and a very irate gunman at an IRA checkpoint giving me a bollicking for driving too fast. Drunk or sober, the rule was to proceed with great caution.

After the Miami disaster, it was excruciating to see a red light being waved in the distance. That was how those poor guys were hoodwinked that fateful night and there was no knowing when it would happen again. There was no way a stop sign could be ignored, and there was also no way of determining the legality or otherwise of the intrusion.

But there was one night on Achill Island when things got as dangerous for Gerry, the roadie, as they ever would in the North. The band played in the local hotel and after the show, the liquor flowed. We drank until the early hours and the hotelier decided that enough was enough.

As Bill and I were falling into my brother Gerry's car, we noticed a woman getting into the front of the brand new Transit van along with the road manager's assistant, a lad by the name of Bat. The irate brother claimed that this was the very lady he had been plying with porter for the best part of the night, and now she was being inveigled to sin with another. She wasn't, but our outrage knew no bounds.

Hardly able to see, we gathered bricks and stones from the home extension site, where the brother's car was parked and launched them in the direction of the pristine van. We shouted our disgust and disapproval and the noise of the ordnance connecting with the Trannie increased our wrath. We cleared the site of bricks, and when they ran out, we hurled a few stones. The two lads and the terrified female cowered in the front section, until the barrage stopped and we headed back to Dublin, righteousness restored.

Gerry came to Freeney and me the next day to show the damage and I nearly threw up. Jaysus, there were big bumps all over its side; it looked like it had contacted a bad dose of chicken pox. He was justly pissed and announced that Bat had officially retired his post.

Sometimes there was a lighter side to our Northern travels. On occasion, we had an extra guitar player, Bobby Kelly, stand in with us to make up the numbers when the promoter specified how many people he wanted in the band. This man had played with Stepaside, a major attraction in Dublin, and was a star in his own right but, on no account would he cross the border.

There was a fairly big gig coming up and we spent a lot of time assuring him there was nothing to worry about, and it was probable that the band would travel up and never even see a policeman, soldier or paramilitary. That's the way it is, we swore, it's just like playing in Kilkenny. We managed to allay his fears and off we set to our gig in the North.

Five men travelled in one of the old, wide, Ford Cortinas and as soon as we drove down the hill at the border town of Newry and turned up the canal, two jeeps of paras, faces blackened and armed to the teeth, pulled alongside and swerved straight in front of our car. They jumped out and, amidst excited roaring and shouting, indicated that we were to get out and stand with our hands against the wall. The officer kept repeating that we were not to speak and the troop made us stand quietly and wait to be questioned.

Two of them took position and called me forward first.

"Name?"

"Where are you going?"

"Where are you coming from?"

"What time did you leave?"

"Why are you going there?"

After answering to his satisfaction, the officer motioned me further up the wall, and ushered the next man up.

It was all very tense and hostile and it appeared they believed they had come across a carload of their sworn enemy.

Bobby was called up and was visibly shaking.

The English accent barked out the same questions he had asked us all, and when our quaking guitar man had finished, he made to move off and join us against the wall.

The Officer shouted "WAIT!" and the bould Bobby replied immediately, "Ten and a half stone."

The troop, the band and the man in charge bent double with laughter. He was a skinny guy, for sure, and terrified, but that afternoon he had the soldiers and us all in hysterics. We laughed all the way to the gig. Things were a lot more serious on the way home, trying to keep her between the hedges whilst anticipating a sight of the dreaded red light signalling us to stop.

But there were more malign forces afoot. The constant travelling, drinking, and lack of sleep was taking its toll on Billy's health. He developed pancreatitis, which subsequently resulted in him becoming diabetic, and the medical people outlined a strict regime for his future conduct. He was shown how to inject himself with insulin and strongly advised to adopt a healthy lifestyle, with complete abstinence from alcohol, except perhaps for a glass or two of wine at Christmas.

He had remarried some time before, and was the proud father of two young daughters, when the condition first began to play havoc with his lifestyle. He couldn't stop drinking water and was putting on serious weight and, to tell the truth, we were relieved that he wasn't more seriously ill. He had been a healthy guy up to this unwelcome darkness and it was the first time any of us had been troubled in any serious way with a health issue. It was as if you expected these things to happen to others, and not to men who were busily engaged in rocking and shocking the nation.

I had diligently learned how to perform an emergency injection of the hormone, in case he went into sugar emergency or if his blood glucose levels got out of kilter, but there was a real fear of the needle. It's strange how the thought of inserting a needle into a person's skin, to save their life, could so frighten a big noisy man, but it did.

The ideal lifestyle, I suppose, for a diabetic would have been anything other than playing in a wild travelling band, with its irregular sleep patterns and meals. Additionally, a balanced mindset would be a powerful asset to a stringent routine and, if coupled with a stress-free employment, then there was a chance of adhering to these new and revolutionary rules of engagement.

He was a dab hand in the kitchen and never needed a recipe book, and thought nothing of arriving home in the middle of the night and changing into his shooting gear and heading off to Dundalk to worry geese. Lying on damp ground for a couple of hours after singing, autographing, snoozing in one car and then driving his own, was enough to test the best. I know many diabetics who live very successful and competitive lives, top people in many disciplines, who manage their lives with discipline, strength and courage, but being a rock icon in Ireland, with its attendant grief, was a long way away from a normal existence, if such a thing exists at all.

He tried hard, of course, to live to the tempo of this new beat, but it was close to impossible to sustain. Driving home transformed the car into a torture chamber. Every time we went over a bump in the road, he would wince, if the pancreatitis was playing up and if whatever painkiller he was on wasn't doing its job. Often, the journey would be prefaced by swallowing, in one gulp, a naggin of whiskey, or some such, and then going into a semi-coma in the back seat.

I remember one night we were coming back from the west and had planned to break the journey in the Longford Arms Hotel, and, more importantly, to refill empty bellies with some much needed juice. Midway through a heavy session, he decided he needed an injection to balance the forbidden stuff on the table, so he limped off, none too steady, in the general direction of the toilets, which was a fairly normal place to do the business.

Shortly afterwards, a busload of American tourists, just up from Shannon airport, arrived at the door and as we were blankly staring at the horde of big fat, green-trousered men and women at check-in, no one noticed that time had passed and Bill wasn't back.

She came screaming out of the Ladies' pisser: "Harry, Harry, there's a junkie in the rest room. He's asleep on the seat and there's a needle stuck in him."

Harry was either the poor husband or tour manager, but we didn't need him. A couple of us got our man revived and, arriving in a coma in Maynooth, managed to wake his nightmare and put him into his own jalopy, which he drove through the quiet Kildare countryside, the half-hour or so, back to Johnstown.

We would then continue on to the city, marvelling at his condition but ignoring our own. We'd laugh and comfort ourselves with talk about him being a wild man, but in truth it was handy to have someone you could call worse than yourself. Billy's main problem was a debilitating, physical ailment; mine was all in the head. The drunken demons of night-time would become agitated again each new day, and demand more liquid thrills to sate their mania. In other words, I awoke gagging, dry-retching, heaving, and hoping I could remember where I had something stashed.

Coming to the end of my time with Yvonne, I used to leave something or other, usually vodka, in the boot of the car. It was too dangerous to take it inside, as she would have thrown it down the sink. And anyone who attacks the precious stash becomes the enemy.

There was always an excuse for going out to the motor "to check something" and it must have looked ridiculous to anyone in the neighbourhood to see this big strange, shaking man stick his head into the arse of his car, turn and twist over onto his side and drain the bottle. It was a wretched start to the day, but a necessary one. It stopped the shaking and neck-twitching, plus it allowed for a bit of social interaction in the house, which would hopefully hide the insanity and help repair the damage. It never did.

It there was no booze at home or in the car, then the journey down to the local bar in Terenure involved a pantomime of pathetic proportions. It always seemed to be just before the start of the holy hour when I got in and ordered a pint of beer, which, I imagined, was some kind of abstemious declaration to the uninterested barman. I was choking for a large vodka, but couldn't order that particular potion because then it would seem that I was a serious victim and actually needed the stuff. It wouldn't be right to order a double straight off. In showbusiness, good impressions are everything. Couldn't have the publican putting it about that you were a lush.

As soon as I'd put my hand out to lift the big glass, it would start to shake. I wouldn't risk the embarrassment of spilling the fuckin' thing all over the counter in an effort to get some of it down, so another strategy was engaged. Getting the shaking hand holding the glass up to your mouth was one peril, but an even greater threat came from the nose. As soon as it sniffed the poison, it would send emergency signals to the brain, which immediately began a ritual, known to all hard-drinking men as the neck-shaking shuffle. The nerves in my collar would make it impossible to steady my mouth, and get the bastard gear in. This physiological masterpiece of placement, the Creator's design, has it this way – with the nose above the mouth, so it can detect damaging stuff about to enter. It works well generally, but when the need is more than a requirement, it can, and must, at all costs, be bypassed.

It is at this stage of desperation that food will make you throw up. Nothing healthy can be tolerated by a system in revolt for sickness. Not that there would be any desire, mind you, but I often found myself compromised at a table, on occasions, before there was a chance of liquid salvation. The food will pass the nose, but be rejected immediately by the Chief Erupter, impatiently awaiting his toxic venom.

Leaving the unsipped pint on the counter, I'd fly across the road to the little off-licence and engage in another charade with the server.

"Aye, there you are, can I have a naggin of vodka please?"

As the thing was being paid for I'd come out with, "She's having a party tonight, and asked me to get this for her, sure she doesn't take much, ha ha."

That might have worked once a year, but it was stretching it to repeat this sorry tale a couple of times a week. The regular lady used to reach for it when she saw me coming, so she had no doubts who the restoration was for. I'd force it down my neck in the jacks of the pub, gagging, heaving, spilling a bit, but getting most of it down. Then it was just a matter of wiping dry the eyes, ditching the bottle, striding out into the lounge bar, and with a loud, confident salutation to the barman, grasp the pint with a near steady hand, and sink it.

"Ah, that oul pint's freezin', Pat, give us a double vod," was the usual carry-on. And the mad head went into the ring for one more unwinnable round with King Alcohol.

I had never heard nor read the Japanese proverb, "Man takes a drink, drink takes a drink, drink takes the man", and I was being taken somewhere bad; going nowhere fast.

Then, after leaving the pub, I had to get out of circulation as soon as possible and get back to the house with a bottle of something to keep the thing going. I tried not to talk to anyone on the street before I got to the car, because there was a fair chance I'd want to cry. If someone came up to me and spoke, or asked about the band, I would have to fight imminent breakdown and collapse.

The little voice in my head was telling me that this bollix is only asking me about the band because he really wants to talk to me about the drinking, about being a bad father and all sorts of wild dementia. I couldn't buy into the idea that he was just a friendly guy who wanted to talk.

Just as the food would be rejected before the poisonous replenishment, so was friendship and love. Any kindness was rewarded with suspicion and love couldn't be tolerated on any account. The few people who cared enough to risk mentioning this mad behaviour with alcohol would be attacked without mercy. You could have criticised my singing, the band, my car, my style, my anything, and I would have laughed it off. But the minute you alluded to the booze, I'd be gone and so would you. I couldn't even take a joke about it, for I believed deep down that it was killing me, yet the thought of giving it up was too horrific to contemplate, or make fun of. It has been described as the merciless obsession that some pursue to the gates of insanity or death; I was hovering in and out of the former, and getting very near the latter. But still, there was no way I'd even consider abstention; I'd rather make a pact with the devil and surrender an arm, or perhaps a leg, as long as I could carry on. Guilt, remorse, shame, fear and a feeling of impending doom were the ever-present headlice of my soul, and every day I awoke, there was a feeling of disappointment, a sort of "Oh Jaysus, not again, where can I get one to get started?"

I had met and spoken to the couple of guys who came to meet me at my ex-wife's behest, and was impressed with their sincerity. But listening to them, it was obvious that these men had a serious problem with liquor and I agreed that it was a good idea for them to give it up.

Life had now become a complete act. I started to pretend that I remembered the events of the previous night and when the lads in the band spoke about plans I'd made for something or other, I nodded sagely, not recalling a thing.

We now drove to gigs in a big American dream car, which seated seven in comfort. It had bench seats and used to kind of float on air to the gigs, and made it a bit more bearable for Billy. It floated in a different fashion on the way home, and many nights I drove with one eye closed to cancel out the second white line on the road. When the double vision got too bad, I allowed one of the men to take over, insisting that I was just tired, and settling back to suck a bottle of something or other until blackout.

Some dawns, I used to come to my senses outside the house I was renting with a pain in my face. Years later, Paddy Freeney told me he used to give me a couple of digs as payback for his frustration and terror in the car and the hassle that would inevitably have occurred at the gig. And he's not what you would call a fighting man.

One Sunday night, when we weren't working, Billy and I were engaged in a session in a Dublin pub. We were concerned with the shortage of gigs and a general lack of funds and the rising debt we were accumulating. As the drink flowed, we mused that there were now only three of the original line-up left: himself, Sean and me. The rest of the lads were paid a set fee per gig and we divvied out what was left after expenses. The resolution to our problem was simple. Sack Sean, and then divide it between the two of us only. It made perfect sense in a drunken haze and we rang him, there and then, from the boozer. Naturally the man was shocked, but the greed had spoken; there was no going back, it was a cruel, done deal.

Mr Karma was up writing, all night.

Paul Claffey was now in charge of our fortune. He lived in Castlerea in County Roscommon and told us that the biz could be done again if we put our minds to it. I don't think he was aware that I had nearly lost whatever mind I had, but he was convinced that the Freshmen could be a major drawing band once more. Oliver's organisation was becoming bigger and he was concentrating more and more on big international concert promotions and Sweepstakes adventures. Besides, I believe he had had just about enough of the madness and didn't want the hassle from ballroom promoters any more.

Claffey was aware of our reputation and lay down, as a condition, that we would fulfil any bookings he got us. That might seem a moderately reasonable request, but there had been many winter nights when we would set off to a gig and, stopping for gut fuel en route, decide that we had gone far enough. The weather was too bad, the car was not going to make it, or the promoter was a bollix anyway. It was never, "we're too pissed to continue".

These were the days before mobile phones and

instant access to all and sundry, so there was no way for the abandoned roadie and whoever he had with him in the van to know if we were coming or not. He would have the gear set up, with the disco or relief band blasting away and the promoter agitating about our pending no-show.

Roadie Gerry Crinnion had left with Oliver and we were using a guy who we called Frank. I didn't know his real name, and he earned the moniker from his uncanny resemblance to a portly television detective who was popular at the time.

Claffey insisted on us shaping up, and for a while it worked. He urged us to get a new roadie and, as a result, we met one of the greatest stars the Freshmen ever produced, Mr Michael Doolin. Claff was filling the book and Mick was getting the band there and running a very tight show. He had an assortment of helpers travel to all the gigs and used his army experience to marshal the troops at every turn. Sometimes he would arrive at a gig with more workers in the van than dancers in the hall, and there was no chance of deliberately missing a gig with this man at the helm. He'd come gunning for you, for sure.

The first night I met him he advised of the following state of affairs in the world:

> Some people make things happen
> Some people watch things happen
> Some people don't know what's happenin'.

Jaysus Mickey, I thought to myself, if only you knew, and it was obvious listening to this magic man the category he chose for himself.

We decided to brighten up proceedings and took on two beautiful girl singers, Imelda Guilfoyle and Frances Rosato. They lit up the scene in their St Trinnian's school uniforms and could sing a bit too, but the sacking virus was still in the air. Frances lasted longer than her companion, but she, for all her talent, fell victim to the bug.

EIGHTEEN

Susie Q

There had been no work for about two weeks, during which time I'd been drinking worse than ever. I vaguely remembered being in Paddy's house with a lady friend and hearing of a gig somewhere outside Cork on the coming Thursday. We didn't normally socialise, but on this particular night I couldn't get back to my flat, as I was too drunk.

The drummer had a key to my place for some strange reason and walked in on the Thursday around noon and asked if I was in any fit condition to travel. I had forgotten about the gig and he continued talking about it and said there were some conditions attached to my travelling. When he called, I was sticking my tongue into the neck of a vodka bottle, hoping against hope for a taste, a hit, something to take away the remorse.

"The promoter wants a six-piece, and you must

be in it. If you're not, there's no gig, but if you drink before or during, there's no deal with the rest of us. I'll drive and we pick up two buskers in Naas who are making up the numbers. If you don't drink as instructed, I will give you a bottle of vodka, immediately afterwards, and plus, there's sixty quid in it. The other lads are going with Mickey; are you on?"

I was flat broke with no sign of anything on the horizon and this was going to be tough but, fuck it, there was money and drink at the end of it.

To the day I die, I shall never forget the journey to Millstreet. We picked up the two session men in Naas, as arranged, but I was unable even to say hello. For the 180 odd miles, all I could do was stare out the windscreen like a zombie and hope my heart would stop pounding in my shirt. Paddy was keeping the show on the road, chatting to the two newcomers, telling them about our programme and what to expect at the gig, but I was on another planet. I tried to turn around, at least to be civil to these friendly men, but I couldn't. It was a mixture of the shakes, fear, embarrassment and exhaustion. I thought the journey would never end, and floated in and out of reality, now and then picking up the sound of laughter from the lads before drifting back to the wilderness.

When I went onstage that night, I believed it was going to be my last night on earth. My eyes were swollen and sore, while the back of my head was throbbing at intermittent speeds. For a minute, the pulse was hardly noticeable, and the next, it battered the skull, speeding up until I believed it must crack free. Then it would subside and revert to the irregular downbeat, beating time with my racing heart. I hadn't eaten in about three days and trying to drink anything was a major ordeal. I did sip a glass of cold water, but spilt more than I drank. My brain was barely aware of the band behind me and they, in turn, were wondering if I would make it to the end. I think the thought of the liquor on the way home kept me going.

Normally, if a man has a headache or other pain before going on to perform, it disappears for the duration of the show. Adrenalin pumps the pain away until the blue light is switched off and normal life resumes. But on this occasion there was no reprieve, and if ever a man worked on autopilot, it was me that night.

Finally the last song was sung and we struck up the national anthem. I stood beside someone I'd never met before as he played it, suffering through its refrain, thinking it would never end, they must be playing it twice, to spite me. Thunder and lightning bolts were destroying my wits and whatever else was functioning in my shaking frame. The longest mile is the last mile home and this time it just seemed to last forever. I could taste the vodka and knew it was the only thing to stop this hammering in my head.

Paddy stood up from the kit and approached and as I stared out of my nearly closed eyes, he asked, "Well, do you want that bottle now?"

Unforgettable words escaped my mouth, and I couldn't believe what I said. "Naw, fuck it Paddy. I just want to get back to Dublin and get a sleep."

It came out entirely on its own. One second, one nano-second beforehand, I was panting, the next I was turning it down. There was no gun to my head, and the thing was on offer, but I said no. I couldn't believe my mouth. I repeated again that I didn't want the poison, and although I can't say I felt good about it, I was convinced. Something mysterious was going down in my head, the "I've had enough switch" had been flicked on in the most unexpected location and circumstance. It wasn't me talking but the words were strong. The amazed drummer said nothing but didn't repeat the invitation.

That was a long, long time ago, and I haven't had a drink since. Trying to lick the inside of the vodka bottle that Thursday morning was my last taste of alcohol, and that excruciating trip to County Cork was the last time I had to endure the punishment it doles out to boys like me. I still had the expedition; the 180 miles back to Dublin, but so had the rest of the lads, and although the mind was still partially detached from my body, I wasn't drunk, and although I didn't know it that night, I would never get pissed again.

It was like starting all over again. I couldn't get used to waking up without a hangover, and I couldn't get used to going to sleep without being blacked-out. I couldn't get to sleep, period, but that was down to drinking gallons of coffee throughout the day. There are people who preach that coffee is just as harmful as booze, but they never wore my shoes, and up to the present I've never had to heave and retch to get the first mocha down.

We had played a cabaret lounge in Castlebar a couple of weeks before Millstreet and ended the night with the clubbers dancing on the tables. We went down a bomb and the crowd loved every minute of it. Some of the lads must have been sober, enough of them anyway to make it count, and we were scheduled to reappear in the western venue about three weeks into the new routine. Going onstage sober was something really new for me and I was hoping for a repeat performance. But it fell flat; I couldn't get the thing into gear at all.

My head was telling me to cop on, to realise that the wild receptions, the roars for more at the end were a thing of the past. You needed to be stoned to get that reaction, it told me, and I might as well give it up, but I had a feeling this couldn't be true. And it wasn't. I met a few lads who had given the stuff up, men who were trudging the journey back to sobriety – musicians, painters, writers, circus performers – and they all reassured me that anything a man can do drunk can be done twice as well sober.

And that proved to be the case. I gradually worked my way back up to ground level, which is a mighty long way from the pits. It didn't stop there and soon began to climb a bit higher and, in no time at all, I found I was enjoying what I discovered at this new altitude. I had completely forgotten about the music itself being the greatest drug of all to a performer. This was something to hang onto.

One of the first things I discovered was that I wasn't the only victim. I was sharing the stage with some very strange men indeed.

The band was a five-piece, and was the tightest outfit we had since Freshmen 2 and the membership remained more or less the same for our final two years on the road. Billy, Tiger, Paddy, Dizzy, Trevor and myself. That makes six, but Dizzy and Trevor shared the bass work at different intervals.

Some nights some of these men could defrost

windscreens with their breath, and the ice would never form again. It was weird to watch the business of serious drinking as a third party and I noted with fascination the personality changes as their intake increased. There didn't seem to be anyone like myself, who got pissed every night, but they seemed to take it in turns to put on the ga-ga.

Having a reputation for doing crazy things came in handy every so often with the crowds, so they didn't seem to mind the action one night in Clogherhead, County Louth. One of the guitar players, a very fiery man, took to heart my criticism of his hero, the legless World War Two pilot Douglas Bader, who I cruelly referred to as the "stumpy bomber". It was a wind-up, but our man took it to the depths of his drunken heart, and halfway through the first set I heard a guitar slide to the floor, string side down. As I looked round to check if all members were still standing, tiny childlike fists rained down on my head. Our man was frothing at the mouth and determined to defend his hero's honour, and the crowd out front laughed themselves silly. Later in the show, when the paying customers had started dancing, he took an interesting solo, propping himself up against his speaker cabinet, which he had mounted on a chair. Midway through the stutterin' licks, the whole ensemble collapsed onto the boards, with our man on top. It was just one of those nights.

The interesting thing about all this is that the following night, when I picked up our suffering soloist, I was forced to administer the Oliver Barry lecture about not drinking before the show and trying to keep the thing half-right.

He looked at me and listened in, shall I say,

disbelief. It was a major role-reversal and he tried the best he could not to burst into laughter. The lads believed that it was only a matter of time before I'd return as King of the Pissheads, so they nodded approvingly and with some degree of glee when I donned the holy vestments. I knew first-hand what Maurice had been up against.

The "Jim Reeves syndrome" had attacked again and a very young Louis Walsh, who seemed to be about ten the first time Billy and I spoke to him in a Dublin bar, replaced Paul Claffey. The man who would go on to greater things was a firm believer in the Brown fellow. But the maestro was getting well past his best in the performing stakes; it would have been impossible to demand more of his weakening frame.

We filled the halls one more time, and Billy was writing through the pain, and it was in this period that he produced his greatest songs.

After a gig one night, he casually invited me to listen to one and, as usual, downplayed it, as just something he had "thrown together".

He sang "Cinderella".

Not for the first time, with this incredible man, I was transported. It was a masterpiece and he rendered it with a tenderness and breath control that would have befitted a command performance, never mind an empty hall in the west of Ireland at three in the morning.

The piano-rolled intro and its beautiful opening couplet heralded a real treat in store:

> I'm a one-fingered piano player,
> Never had much time for music's heavy side

Might have listened to Beethoven,
Or played some Chopin in my time.

It was spellbinding; it made my flesh tingle and goose
pimples run down my spine. He sang like a man who
knew he had been granted a fabulous gift, yet hadn't
made the most of it, but with this creation he would
start paying his dues. It was the music of a great
composer, stating that his soul had been sold once
too often, but that now this was an earnest attempt at
redemption, a bruised and broken celebration of his
defeat – one that would tolerate no compromise. The
long, delicate fingers that had raped the piano keys
that day long ago in Trench House in a thunderous
assault now seduced beautiful, hypnotic sounds from
the ivories, accompanying his:

> I wish you could have seen me, diggin'
> Rossini,
> Most beautiful sounds, beyond my wildest
> dreams.

Once again, out of the blue, after nearly twenty years
together, in bands of varying ability, this beautiful
man thrilled me to the marrow.

If you die before hearing "Cinderella", you have
lived in vain. If you have ever loved and lost, it will
heal you. It is one of the great classic songs of our
time, and it was never released commercially.

That night, on the way home from the gig, I
asked the great man if he would sing it in the act.
He assured me he would, but no matter how many
times I tried, it was never done. Sinatra would have
made it number one worldwide, but he was denied

the pleasure.

One ditty he did perform and had a hit with was his glorious punk satire "I've Never Heard Anything Like It". The late John Peel, who interviewed the Larne man and spoke about him for months afterwards, made it Record of the Month on his BBC show. But it wasn't properly promoted internationally, primarily because of Billy's deteriorating health, although there was one overnight trip to sing it on Dutch TV.

Tiger wrote a powerful rocker, which we put out along with the punk send-up and he called it "Bombing Run" after his great legless hero. It too was a bit of a hit.

These songs got the country talking again and the big American car, which we had named "Rhonda", was rarely off the road. We even had it insured properly in the category reserved for travelling one-night stands. It was strange to be sober and in charge of myself, but it was no pleasure to see the mounting woes of our Creator in Chief.

We had travelled to Carrick-on-Shannon in County Roscommon for a Sunday night carnival, and entering the residents' lounge for a cup of brew before the gig, I saw her. She sat in an armchair with a bandana on her soft blonde hair, and was the most beautiful woman ever to grace my eyes. It was impossible to do anything other than stare, but having made eye contact, she quickly looked away. But it was enough to encourage.

"Can I get you a drink?"

"No thanks."

Retreating happily, for I had, by now, looked right into her gorgeous face, I determined to ask again at half-time of the football game that she was watching on the TV.

"Will you have that drink now, then?" I inquired again, at the anointed hour.

"No thanks," but this time, I caught a glimpse of a smile, a heart-warming sign.

At full-time, I decided to have one last go, and if she refused I'd let it go reluctantly, and I would annoy this vision no more.

"Are you sure you wouldn't like a drink?"

"You're not going to give up, are you?" was the smiling reply and thus was born an unmissable adventure with the great love of my life, the beautiful Susan Kelly.

If quitting the poison was the thing that saved my life, this woman was the reason to live it. I fell completely beneath her charming spell and she introduced me to a love and a love of life that lingers in my soul. She was only twenty-three at the time and was really into the music, and she had never heard of the Freshmen. That night at the dance, I sang my heart out and every song was aimed in her direction. It seemed to work for we arranged to meet the following night in Mullingar.

Over dinner the following evening, she wondered why I wasn't partaking of the wine. She laughed when I told her that I was "compromised" in that area, and it didn't take many words to get the situation across. She didn't mind one tiny bit. This was Heaven.

I had been told by friends and read many times that as one door closes, another opens; if you can hold the head, and do the next right thing. But this was opening the double doors to a palace, with scented stairways, manned by host of smiling angels. I fell in love that night in Carrick and the barometer never went down. It would go missing on a few occasions, but it still registered somewhere on the scale from very comfortable to super hot, when all was said and done.

Time was running out for Bill. I believe he used the road gigs to escape from the discipline he had at home, but these diversions were becoming very painful. Apart from hard-sung vocals and driving a piano for two hours, the roll-ups and the naggins were jolting his pendulum too far wide off its normal swing.

He did a bit of writing for various magazines, reviewing latest releases and some radio shows and record production, but, after wildlife, painting had become his major retreat.

Like anything he turned his hand to, the man excelled and was represented by a gallery in Naas which sold his work as soon as it arrived from his studio. There never seemed to be a day when it was comfortable for him and it was clear that the day was fast approaching when he would have to quit the road.

History was repeating itself, for once again he was beginning to miss out on a lot of dates, but this time around it stemmed from a weakened body, not a broken heart. The promoters weren't happy with a four-piece and relations with them became acrimonious. It was hard to blame them, for they had advertised Billy Brown, Derek Dean and the Freshmen, and, as they saw it, they had been served half-measures.

It was with a degree of relief that I listened to his voice on the phone, one Monday afternoon, telling me that he could go on no further. He couldn't take it anymore and, besides, he had been asked by Johnny Logan to work for a couple of months as musical conductor in TV stations throughout Europe, promoting his Eurovision winner, "What's Another Year". We had a good laugh when he asked rhetorically, "Do you think I should take it, Bigman?"

We continued on, playing a six-week circuit in various guises and degrees of sobriety. Men offered their services and learned the set en route to the gig. But it was becoming very clear that there was no future in it for anyone; the magic was gone, the halls were too small, and the road too narrow. We agreed to work the Christmas and see where we were in the New Year, but although we had a decent dairy it was more and more of the same old stuff.

Christmas 1980 was a soggy plod for a four-piece and the crowds had just about heard enough. We travelled to Boyle, near Carrick-on-Shannon, on New Year's Eve and when we set out from Dublin it was obvious there would be nobody at the dance. The roads were deserted and covered in ice. It was a treacherous journey and, when we arrived, Mickey D had the gear set up and ready.

"Not be too many tonight, Bigman."

About fifty hardy souls attended the wake of the Freshmen, that cold and bitter night, and we played the two hours or so until the staff opened the side doors to the freezing night air. There were no photos, autographs, encores or big announcements to the paltry, half-frozen crowd.

It wasn't part of any plan, there was no definite decision that we would throw in the towel, but that night in Roscommon we put her to bed.

Epilogue

It was a young enough age to become a has-been. Thirty-eight is not exactly the flowering of youth, but my mind was clear. I had been there, seen that, rode the T-shirt and seen the video and, what's more, I was convinced that this very new field, video production, would elevate me to superstar status in the business world. It never occurred to the much-depleted mass of nervous tissue I called a brain that some kind of training, experience or guidance would be necessary; it was just going to be a simple matter of making a few connections and having the right idea. It was only a matter of time until I became one of the nation's leading industrialists and experts would seek my advice. I wasn't short on self-confidence.

Paddy and I talked about future developments in the video world. Instead of going out to the cinema, people would stay at home and watch the latest movies on their own TV. There weren't any movies on video in 1981, at least in Ireland, and there was a distinct absence of video players, but none of that mattered. We were going to become leaders in the field, and it would mushroom and grow until we conquered the world.

I bought a dozen video players and tried to sell them door to door, but it was like selling airbags for pushbikes. A good idea but a bit ahead of its time. They haven't gotten round to the two-wheel protection cushions yet, but you can be sure someone is thinking about it. There was a half-hearted attempt to become the Cecil B De Mille of the video-wedding industry, but the same story held true. People had no idea what I was talking about. It was a good idea, they agreed, but when and where could they play it.

I began looking for movies on video cassettes, but there was very little available from the major studios. We rented a few, but gave up on the idea as we couldn't fulfil the demand without bootlegged copies of dubious quality and origin. There was a limit to the number of times even the most dedicated, strung-out film junkie could watch *The Sound of Music*.

Suffice to say that I had Susan's head turned with grand ideas and after my failure to set the world alight in the home entertainment arena, I became involved in selling Spanish property. That went well until there was a crash in the market all over Europe and it all ended amid much hullabaloo.

Turning my sights now on the invention market, I began to design machines, which, at the touch of a screen, and some information from the customer, would print out a guide for future life choices. It failed when the investors baulked at the last moment, but the idea was sound and actually appeared a few years later. I just didn't have the necessary skills to make it happen.

And so I returned to the has-been, nearly-man, once again, and my next assignment was a weekly trip to Werburgh Street in Dublin 1, to sign on and collect whatever largesse the State had on offer. I was absolutely flat broke.

I felt Mr Karma was being a bit unfair, but he's a hard fucker to please when you're entered on the wrong side of his ledger too many times.

It was some culture shock. It was deflation of ego in depth, and standing in one of several long lines of fellow-signatories, the devaluation of my currency as a "big operator" was most convincingly rammed home.

"Sing now, ya boy ya" took on a whole new meaning and as I stood at the top of the line of desperate men, the very first time, waiting for the lady to access my card from her file, I gave her a big smile and cracked a corny joke. The pencil was tied onto the grill bars of the little cubbyhole she peeped out of, and I wasn't too sure if I should tell her that I used to sign autographs for girls like her, but thankfully I kept my mouth shut, did the biz, and moved on. There were a lot better men than me standing waiting to be served and besides, there was no room for self-pity, only gratitude. Sure I was able to do it without needing a drink, and a man had to be grateful for that.

"Welcome to the real world, Big Derek; this is where boys like you end up," was the nagging mantra of Mr Negativity in the back of my head, but I told the fucker to shut up and drove into town for a coffee.

The following week I overslept and called the dole office to apologise and the very nice man at the other end of the phone assured me that there was no problem; just to come in the next day at eleven and harmony could be restored.

The place was bedlam and so noisy that it resembled a gig when we were at our loudest. Big men were roaring across the trench lines at one another and they all seemed to be stuck to the man in front of them in the line. They were all lining up the way a cold man holds onto his warm wife in the middle of the night, after getting in from a freeze. There were a few security staff, something I had not noticed on my previous visit, at the front of the building, and the street outside was chock-a-block with Hiace vans, filled with stern-faced women waiting for their men to come outside and hand over. At least that's what I thought, as I observed this arrangement on the way in.

I stood in line, and immediately felt another man spoon right up tight against me. He was, as they say in Dublin, "bet into me". I was, by extension, bet into the lad in front, and in this fashion the travelling conga inched forward. I was somewhere in the middle of the line and the only thing missing was a band playing and our legs being kicked in unison. The mighty big man, whose posterior I was in danger of pushing out through the front of his zipper, craned his neck and shouted at me, "Are ye goin' to the weddin?"

"When's it on?" I asked for fear of offending him.

"Friday, for fuck's sake; don't ye know, it's a three-caker."

We shouted a conversation of sorts until we reached the hutch, and he signed and was off. He was a happy man and the only friendly face I ever met down in Werburgh Street, where heads, in the main, hung low. It would have been easy to start a revolution down here, I used to think; there were hundreds of fit and hungry men. But before it started, another career, doing something or other, came along. I went from attending FÁS courses to running them. And there were all sorts of gigs in between. FÁS is a training and employment body established by the Irish government to broaden the skills base in the workforce, and I, for one, was very glad of its help.

That's what was happening when someone suggested a revival. Freshmen mark 24, and I freely went along with the idea of doing it again. But it didn't work, they rarely do, and we scrapped the venture after a couple of gigs. No matter how you dress up yesterday's helpings, the fresh fish is always preferable. As with fish, so with men; we'd had our day, and now it was time for the young bucks to rear their head.

Billy's painting and recording kept him in the public eye and we stayed in touch occasionally. He played piano in a couple of venues and lived a life much more conducive to an unhealthy man trying to stay fit. He continued writing beautiful songs and produced records for many of our leading acts.

Sean established a business in the North that became a major success. He operates Shawson Supply, which services the diesel-engine market and does it with all the skill and dedication he so enthusiastically gave to the band.

Paddy runs Litton Lane Studios, a powerhouse in the National PA business in Ireland and works, occasionally, as tour manager for Van Morrison.

Tiger still plays and teaches young men and women the beauty and joy of the guitar, and it was a special thrill for me to bring my first-born son Jamie for his first guitar lesson to a man I consider simply the best. The hair isn't as bushy these days, but the eyes still have that dangerous look about them.

I have no relationship with the other lads, and except for meeting them all a few years ago, on the band's last get-together, I have never seen or spoken to any of them.

The only reason I agreed to do the reunion in the Waterfront Hall, Belfast in 1999 was for posterity. The BBC recorded one of the five nights live and I wanted something of the old days for, well, the old days' sake. The shows went really well, but also reaffirmed my belief that once it's over, you should let it go. The crowds loved it and the serpent had a special outing one evening all to himself, but there was something missing. It was the blue energy, the light, the kundalini, the youth, the danger, the lust, the hunger, and all like things that young men have, and middle-aged men foolishly imagine they retain.

We sang the right notes in the right places, but it was not the right time. In an interview between shows, the BBC asked me what would be my main memory of the series, and I answered without hesitation. I said it had to be standing on the same stage as Billy Brown one more time. I felt like saying one last time, for it was obvious to all he was in desperate physical shape even though his spirit battled to shine through.

He had called me a couple of months previously and arranged to come to my Dublin cottage for a chat. He didn't say about what, specifically, but it was clear there was something on his mind.

He arrived about midnight and we chatted till dawn. It was the warmest talk we'd ever shared, and at the end of it there were tears in both our eyes. We spoke of love, lack of love, happiness and pain. And we revealed secrets to one another that had been denied the ears of any man, or woman; things I believed would never see the light of day. He laughed when I recalled how much I'd lived in awe of his magic, of how jealous I was of his style, of how he intimidated and inspired me in equal measure. And that was only the beginning.

So, speaking on TV that afternoon in Belfast at the Waterfront, I knew about his spirit; I wasn't talking with an empty head or false heart. He wasn't there to be interviewed, so there was no sense of embarrassment, not that I wouldn't have spoken the same way had he been sitting on my knee.

A short time later, Billy passed away.

The coffin was sitting, alone in the empty funeral home, with the lid closed. I asked the lady in attendance if she would open it and she did so, with reluctance, after proclaiming, "You're the boy he used to sing with."

He lay in peace. His hair was as blond as the first day I'd seen him, and there was an aura of majesty about his slender white face. There was no sign of the horrible, convulsive pain that we'd all seen so often, but there was no wicked gleam either. All I could do was utter a prayer for his soul and for his grieving wife and children. I couldn't speak to him; I was too sad. We had done all the talking anyway, there was nothing more to be said.

We buried him in Glasnevin cemetery and I had the honour of carrying his coffin into the church along with his three fine sons. I recalled how, when I was carrying my own beautiful father's casket to the graveside, Bill had suddenly appeared out of nowhere and put his shoulder underneath the box, as someone else slipped out. He had driven from Dublin to Strabane when he heard about my Dad's demise, and insisted on paying his respects. Billy was that kind of special man. My dear old Dad, like most men, loved this son of Ireland, this Celtic vagabond, and had he been around, I wouldn't have been allowed to carry his corpse to its rest.

The entire original band, with one exception, showed up to share their grief, and a great majority of the other sometime players paid their respects too. It was a sad and bitter day.

It would take another book to tell about the music since then and of the many and unpredictable turns and crossroads my life has enjoyed.

My marriage to Susan ended, yet I didn't have a drink. It was not even a consideration. I was shell-shocked when it happened and thought, once again, that it was the worst day of my life. I believed Mr Karma was calling for the payment of some more dues, and hoped that, if nothing else came out of this newest calamity, his slate would be wiped clean.

I got on with living as best I knew how and then, on one of the many twists, I met Elise, a dark-skinned daughter of a Belgian father and Zairean mother. A doctor in gynaecology, I called her Dr Death and we lived it up as if she was the first love in my life. She had her own business in Brussels and was a senior figure in Belgium's struggle to introduce abortion, hence the moniker. She had been to Ireland only once and had never heard of the Freshmen. She never heard me sing, and I never offered. It lasted just over a year and its rupture was only healed by my meeting Rowena.

Oh, holy Jaysus, another worst day in my life when Elise waved *au revoir* and another "best day ever" when this English damsel flashed her green eyes my way. I had known her husband whilst in the Spanish property biz, but they had separated. Ten years after Jamie was born, young Harvey arrived to fill my life with joy. I don't think it will come as a surprise to learn that this wonderful love didn't last a lifetime either.

I was thinking about good days and bad days when the light went on in my brain that I am the worst possible judge of what is best and what is worst. It was the worst day ever when Yvonne walked out, but it turned out to be the best when Susan walked in. But that, in turn, left me with the worst when Susan went as well, which again, proved really to be a good one when Elise made her entrance. Her departure was definitely the pits, but that was disproved by Rowena's appearance on the scene and her exit seemed to ... you see what I mean? I can't continue as I don't wish to tempt fate, but I think you'll agree that what is considered the end, is just a prelude to a new beginning. And that's the only healthy way to look at the gig. Of course, you could always make your case that I'm not the best man to sustain a relationship with beautiful women, but you'd be wrong. It's them who can't keep it up with me. They just seem to get enough after a couple of years.

I have never lost the wonder of waking up without a hangover. Whenever I'm driving these days and get pulled over by a guard or guardette, I smile a big beamer and think to myself, "You're twenty years too late."

I often think of the night I was driving out of Dublin en route to Clones in County Monaghan. It was a Sunday and I was alone in car, as the other lads had gone ahead with the roadie. The dirty lust was rising like steam from the serpent's head, and I could hardly keep the motor straight such was his need.

She stood alone, majestic and very desirable at the side of the road and this gift from above, wearing tight, white jeans, raised her thumb as I approached. I'd had a few drinks earlier in the day and this was the excuse for a few more.

She got in and immediately recognised her driver and off we sped to the pub and on to Clones. We got high on the scent of what was to come and I couldn't wait for the gig to end, so we could hurry back to the car and celebrate further our instant and compelling love.

I wore tight, brushed velvet trousers onstage and because of the heat they generated, I normally went up, "freeballin'". In case any reader might be confused about the meaning of this state, I'd better explain. You go "freeballin'" when you don't wear drawers. The gonads can bounce any which way. Anyway, the cobra liked room to breathe, and it was a lot cooler. I tell you this because, as soon as the last note was shot, I was down in the crowd and we headed back to Dublin, still wearing the velvet strides and skinny T-shirt.

"Oooh, Derek, I love your trousers, would you give them to me?" she cooed as the anaconda was practically bursting through the weakening velvet.

Trousers, trousers, I thought. At that moment I'd have ripped my heart out and put it in her handbag.

She had her way with the velvet strides, and the reptile had his wicked way with her. As she wriggled her way to the front door, I thought that they looked much better on her, and watched as she blew a lusty kiss before disappearing from view.

A few miles down the road, the nasty realisation that I was driving to Dublin at five in the morning, twenty times over the legal limit and wearing no trousers, dawned alarmingly on my demented head. I sat there, naked, except for a short vest, and the remains of a bottle of unfinished whiskey, and as the terror of being stopped by the cops mounted, all I could do was take a few more swigs.

It was about 50 yards from the car door to the entrance to my flat and my big bare bum covered the distance in record time for a drunk man.

My story is as I remember it, difficult at the best of times, but doubly so due to the never-ending succession of blackouts. No one was taking notes and I'm sure I've left out some of the most important events in the story of the band. If you were to ask what was the most amazing thing in an unforgettable ride of a career, the answer is simple. I survived it.

Leaving the Central Mental Hospital in Dundrum village recently, one of the gatemen approached as I was about to hand in my visitor's pass. I was visiting a friend who ended up there because of his inability to handle the biggest drug in our pleasant land, the booze.

"Good man, Derek, are you doing anything with the band these days?"

"Naw, sure I'm well past it now."

"What are you doin' with yourself then?"

"Actually I'm writin' a book."

"And what's it about?"

"Ah, it's all about women and drink, drink and the women."

"Well, that explains it, no wonder you couldn't sing."

I laughed all the way to the village. There was a smile in my heart.

Discography

45rpm/7″ Singles.

1964: "He's The One You Love"/"I Love My Little Girl" – (Six of One)

1965: "I Stand Alone"/"Gone Away" – (Oriole CD 305)

1965: "La Yenka"/"Don't Say Love" – (Pye 7N15964)

1966: "So This Is Love"/"King Cole Yenka" – (Pye 7N17037)

1966: "Cara Mia"/"Better Believe It" – (7N17230)

1967: "Papa oo Mow Mow"/"Let's Dance" – (Pye 7N 17432)

1968: "Go Granny Go"/"Look At The Sunshine" – (Target 7N17592)

1969: "She Sang Hymns Out Of Tune"/"Mr Beverly's Heavy Days" – (Target 7N 17757)

1969: "Just To See You Smile"/"Indian Lake" – (Target 7N 17689)

1970: "Banquet For The World" / "The Time Is Now"
  – (CBS 5168)

1970: "Halfway To Where" / "Time Hasn't Changed
  Her"– (CBS 4842)

1971: "One Bad Thing" / "Everywhere There Is Love"
  – (CBS 7241)

1972: "Swannee River" / "Take The Time It Takes"
  – (CBS 7694)

1972: "La Linda" / "My Home Town" – (CBS 8079)

1973: "All My Trials" / "Child Song" / "Hold On"
  – (Dolphin DOS104)

1973: "I Found My Freedom" / "Listen To A Country
  Song" – (Dolphin DOS 106)

1974: "What Colour Is God's Skin" / "The Time Is
  Now" – (Dolphin DOS 126)

1974: "Longer Boats" / "Alabama" – (Dolphin DOS
  122)

1975: "Papa oo Mow Mow" / "Northwest Territory"
  – (Hawk HASP375)

1976: "Go Granny Go" / "Carpet Man" – (Dolphin
  DOS137)

1979: "I Never Heard Anything Like It" / "Bombing
  Run" – (Release RL 975)

33.3 rpm/ 12" Albums
1968: *Movin' On* – (PYE NPL 18263)
1970: *Peace On Earth* – (CBS S 64099)
1974: *Now And Then* – (Dolphin DOLB 7015)

**ALSO AVAILABLE FROM MERLIN
PUBLISHING AND WOLFHOUND PRESS
IN ALL GOOD BOOKSHOPS
NATIONWIDE...**

ALWAYS ME
DICKIE ROCK

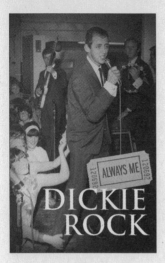

Price: €24.99/Stg£16.99
ISBN: 978-1-903582-74-9
Hardback
Publication: OUT NOW!

MERLIN
PUBLISHING

Always Me tells the remarkable story of Dickie Rock's rise to fame from his first performance as a boy soprano with the local choir in Cabra West, to playing the London Palladium and becoming a '60s sex symbol, blessed with a velvet voice that made the ladies swoon and the men envious.

As lead singer of the legendary Miami Showband, the electric atmosphere of the ballrooms is re-created as Dickie talks about performing in front of thousands of hysterical fans, the other showbands on the scene and the highs and lows of their rollercoaster lifestyle.

Dickie remains one of Ireland's most loved entertainers to this day. In *Always Me* he reveals the many challenges he has faced over the years and the unbearable heartache of the family tragedies behind the success and fame. He also discloses some unforgettable highlights including an encounter with the Mob in New York, representing Ireland at the Eurovision in 1966, entertaining Martin 'The General' Cahill in his dressing-room and giving Cliff Richard a run for his money.

Always Me *is the most revealing insight ever into the man that triggered the women of Ireland to shout: "Spit on me, Dickie!"*

Enquiries to: Merlin Publishing, Newmarket Hall, Cork Street, Dublin 8
Tel/Fax: + 353 1 453 5866/5930   publishing@merlin.ie
www.merlinwolfhound.com

LINES I LOVE
MARY KENNEDY

MERLIN
PUBLISHING

ISBN: 978 1903582 763
Price: €12.99/Stg£8.99
Hardback
Publication: November 2007

"Life is mostly froth and bubble,
Two things stand like stone.
Kindness in another's trouble,
Courage in one's own."

Finding a yellowed, hardback copy-book when she was clearing out her mother's house, Mary Kennedy was surprised to discover a collection of cuttings and thoughts that her Mam had written down, over a number of years. Some of them Mary knew; the moralistic ones were especially familiar, as her Mam had quoted them to her children growing up, but others she had never come across before. The coincidence was that Mary did the same thing.

In Lines I Love Mary Kennedy combines her mother's pieces with her own collection of sayings and quotes which she has built up throughout her life – taking notes from books, gathering pieces of poetry and sayings that all hold some special meaning for her. From childhood poems and adult wisdom, to lines about nature, friendship, death, Africa, children and inspirational women, all the quotes have one thing in common – they make her stop and think.

For all those moments when you're looking for the perfect phrase Lines I Love *will give you just what you need.*

Enquiries to: Merlin Publishing, Newmarket Hall, Cork Street, Dublin 8
Tel/Fax: + 353 1 453 5866/5930   publishing@merlin.ie
www.merlinwolfhound.com

COLOUR FOR LIVING
HOW TO CHANGE YOUR
LIFE WITH COLOUR
TINA DUNNE

Price: €19.99/Stg£13.99
ISBN: 978-1-903582-75-6
Paperback
Publication: Spring 2008

MERLIN
PUBLISHING

In Tina Dunne's *Colour for Living* learn about the importance and impact of colour in our everyday lives.

Colour can sway our thinking, change actions and cause reactions. It can energise you, raise your blood pressure or suppress your appetite! Similarly, when used in the wrong way, colour can contribute to low self- esteem, poor decisions making and fatigue.

Find out more about the positive and negative side of colour as Tina, a consultant nutritionist with a number of health spas and restaurants, takes us through 12 different colour personalities. Learn about how focusing on one particular colour can project a particular self-image and how eating colour related foods can promote well being. Try out Tina's colour coded recipes which will help get you on the road to a positive and healthy lifestyle!

Enquiries to: Merlin Publishing, Newmarket Hall, Cork Street, Dublin 8
Tel/Fax: + 353 1 453 5866/5930   publishing@merlin.ie
www.merlinwolfhound.com